THE SPIRAL OF LIFE

Bridge the Gap
of Your Internal and
External Life with
Tap Around the Clock

Rachel Earing

authorHOUSE®

AuthorHouse™ UK
1663 Liberty Drive
Bloomington, IN 47403 USA
www.authorhouse.co.uk
Phone: 0800.197.4150

Published by AuthorHouse 02/05/2019

ISBN: 978-1-7283-8236-4 (sc)
ISBN: 978-1-7283-8235-7 (e)

CONTENTS

ACKNOWLEDGMENTS

To my gorgeous boys Jack, Charles and Tom.
Love you to the furthest stars and back.

To my loving partner, Bryan, who has been my rock throughout the turbulent changes in my life as I trained to become an Energy Therapist and transformed my life along the way. His silence and strong presence throughout the years has given me a fuller understanding of how time and silence can be the greatest communicators we have to reach within and heal ourselves.

My gorgeous mum and brother Marcus for being my sturdy roots through life. My dad, for being dad, a learning curve in itself, and each and every one of my dear friends and colleagues who have been with me on my journey so far.

I couldn't have got this far without you all. To each and every one of you the following applies:-

Ho' oponopono

Ancient Hawaiian Prayer

I love you
I'm Sorry
Forgive Me
Thank you
Author Unknown

INTRODUCTION

Welcome to "The Spiral of Life" which has been designed to Bridge The Gap between our Logical understanding of Energy Therapy, resulting in an increase in your emotional intelligence and general mental health. This book is a workable tool to use at any time of day or night to start focusing and taking self-responsibility for you and those you care about Emotionally, Physically and Spiritually.

This book is a personal therapists journey to help you can make comparisions of how this works on a day to day, year to year, level of life.

HOW DOES IT WORK?

As I progressed as an Energy Therapist, specialising with families, I soon realised my clients' emotional intelligence was limiting them open up to the truly incredible possibilities that lay ahead of them. To help them increase this awareness I gave them a visual tool to help explain how Energy Therapy works. Thus, the contents of this book are the results of bringing that information together, which all ages, genders and cultures can connect with. It only seemed right to share it, so you may benefit too.

This book contains key information that top Energy Therapists use to free their clients from debilitating emotional and physical conditions, without any intervention from the medical world. IE: no drugs, no needles, no scans, no hospitals, no doctors.

This information has been condensed into 3 workable charts, enclosed (also available in poster size) for quick reference and guidance. The explanations for the methods of using the charts are also on an Apple App, (Tap Around The Clock). It is perfect for Therapists and families to use together and on their own.

Emotional Intelligence - Connecting Mind, Body & Spirit

Emotional intelligence is an awareness of how you connect truly with the communication being sent to you all through your energy system, physically, mentally and spiritually. To show you how to connect these together I have used our meridian system; the 24 hour clock and some of the tapping/holding points from EFT (Emotional Freedom Technique); a guide of what symptoms you may find in each area and how they communicate together. Using all this information together or in parts helps release triggers or blockages such as "anxiety, fear, and headaches". This creates gaps of space within our energy system. This space enables us to take on more freely life's new challenges.

These charts include the following:

> ➢ The Meridian Clock Times
> ➢ The Meridian Areas
> ➢ Some of the Emotions or Physical Ailments in each Meridian
> ➢ The Tapping or Holding points for each Meridian

WHO AM I?

I'm an involved and supportive mum of 3 football mad teenagers, and my beautiful Jack Russell and a loving and involved fiancée, daughter, sister, friend, and a sensory being just like you.

My professional background consists of 20 years at ITV Studios (Granada TV & LWT TV) in both Broadcasting and Production. I then moved into smaller working establishments, firstly, for a cluster of schools then smaller local companies. As time progressed especially with having my own young family, I realised I was more passionate about helping the people I worked with, emotionally and physically, rather than the working environment I'd ended up in.

The result; I am now a Family Energy Therapist, qualified as an Advanced EFT Practitioner, Master NLP Practitioner, Reiki Master and Advanced Diet & Nutrition Coach.

WORKING ON ME

To be an effective, compassionate and understanding Therapist I had to work on myself along the way. You see I'd spent over 30 years feeling guilty, embarrassed, and ashamed at some of the things I'd done, couldn't do or wished I'd done, as some of you may have. (Although, hopefully not for as long as me!)

I've done the waking up at 3am, night after night, trying to work out my problems, plus everyone else's. Fallen asleep just before the alarm goes off, then lifelessly dragged myself to the day's tasks ahead.

I've driven myself crazy, mentally and physically by worrying about the future, fretting about the past, and missing the joy of the moment I was in.

I've been in the position, where I was so eager to experience everything life threw at me, I never stopped long enough to even think about the pattern of events I was going through, again and again and again; just in a different place, with different people, each time.

I worked on the basis that "I'll keep every experience and memory as vivid as possible with me, and then I'll know what to do next time". It turned out that wasn't really working for me; and eventually, I had to take time to look back on past events.

Patterns most definitely had started to unfold, and the lessons had got bigger and bigger over the years. Eventually these lessons nearly engulfed me, drowning me in a downward spiral of depression, disgust and helplessness.

Suddenly, I was a 40+ single mum stuck in a meaningless job, trying to hold my family together, financially struggling and lost emotionally and physically.

I'd started off so well. How did I get so lost?

I finally engaged in what was happening in my life and started to address the issues. My emotional intelligence had dropped to an all time low and I was unable to decipher effectively the simplest of exchanges at home or at work without it causing me or those around me great distress.

I started to change drastically what I was doing and what I was reacting to, not just for me but for the sake of my boys too. I'd been massively aware of the impact the split between my ex-husband and I had had on the boys, and over the years I'd tried every tool I had at the time, to repair the damage or make it better. We'd be ok for a while, and then something would happen usually out of my control and my reactions to it would have no consistency. I'd yo-yo between the new way I should approach things and the old.

When this happened, the frustration of the old pattern kicking back in, especially when I was over tired, stressed and juggling life was the most difficult time of all. I was exhausted, and just couldn't sustain the new pattern of behaviour. It was driving me crazy.

As I delved deeper into energy therapy, I learnt about how our sensory system works with our emotional and physical selves. I learnt that our thoughts impact on our emotions. Our emotions impact on our behaviour and how all of this ripples and impacts on our physical health.

BREAKING IT DOWN

For example, as children our thoughts come through without much of a filter and we act instinctively on what we want. It is only outside factors that let us know if we have gone about it the "wrong/inappropriate" way even if we get the result we initially wanted.

Please note the "wrong" way may never really be "wrong", unless we have broken the law. It may just be that other people let us know their version of what is or isn't appropriate.

This will cause "confusion" inside our energy system as we try to understand why something that feels so right, can then become unacceptable, as we try to please others to fit into our environment.

For example, as a baby we may cry and cry to make sure we get fed or clean. This works, so we continue until the first time we are told otherwise. We may test this many times to see what the results are and we test this using all of our senses to connect with the external world. The feedback we get is how we learn to react in different ways to get the results we want.

SENSORY SYSTEM COMMUNICATION

SO, the first time we ever feel "confused" because we have acted instinctively on getting something we want, our sensory system has a huge RUSH of internal chaos as it processes every sensory detail about "confusion" to our subconscious. Our heart may race. We may start to get hot and sweat excessively, or get a tightness in our body. We also see and hear the impact on others to that event and digest their reactions. All of this happens whilst we logically try to work out how to stop this chaotic feeling inside us and the external events that go with it.

Our whole energy system remembers this chaotic communication and stores it so it can protect us from "Confusion" next time. So, "confusion" may become a trigger in our system, relaying information back to us, saying; "whoah, we didn't like this feeling last time, what can we do to protect ourselves from it"?

"Confusion" may result in us then feeling "guilty" that we don't know how to deal with this problem. This again may become a trigger, as we try to escape this new feeling. Note. negative feelings may put our system into an immediate Fight, Flight or Freeze mechanism if we don't know how to manage them. Fight Flight and Freeze are all safety modes of survival and stop our system from repairing itself, replenishing and moving on if we get stuck there.

If this is the case, we end up with "Layers of Triggers" one on top of another until we learn to deal with them in a positive way. It is only by dealing with them in a positive way that the Fight, Flight or Freeze mechanism disappears, otherwise we are feeding the layers to get bigger and bigger, creating more and more anxiety and stress in our system.

We have the potential to evolve second by second, minute by minute with our unique ability to learn and adapt. What would happen if we learnt to collapse down everyone else's belief on what is "wrong" and learnt to trust ourselves on our inner most, instinctive selves on what is right?

Please do not misinterpret what I mean by this. I do not mean our knee jerk reaction to a situation or a selfish act of just looking out for me, but our deep routed inner most knowing's, which most of us have lost the ability to recognise. It would be like pressing the reset button on a computer but with our emotions, keeping our learned understanding to date but able to react from the emotional place we are now, not the reaction we would have had yesterday or last year. We have all moved on physically, emotionally and spiritually from just yesterday's experiences. What have we, or could we, truly learn from that?

What is the Outside?

The outside is the environmental impacts which affect your life. Ie: everything that comes at you from outside your own energy system and impacts on it. Such as, other people's views and beliefs, food, drink, pollution, school, work, nature, etc.

Tuning into too much of this and taking it on as our own may lead to the start of a SPIRAL to stagnation or stress.

What is the Inside?

The inside is your inner self ie: your unique energy system which is where all your memories are stored from all the chaos of your unique life. It just needs talking to in its own language to give you the answers you seek. This is sometimes known as your "gut instinct", "follow your gut", follow your intuition.

Your vegus nerve connects your gut to your brain and sends a signal from your gut long before our logical brain can work things out. Learning to listen to this is learning about our instincts.

Tuning into this through natural Vibrational Energy resources is the start towards the SPIRAL to success.

Your whole energy system is ready to work with you and it will flow and flow and flow with those answers you've been looking for if you tune in correctly. The lesson is to learn to decipher what to deal with and what to leave alone.

How do we Tap into trusting the Inside?

LAYERS OF TRIGGERS

Let's have a deeper look at Layers of Triggers and what we understand by that.

Here's a little chart to show us how this may progress:-

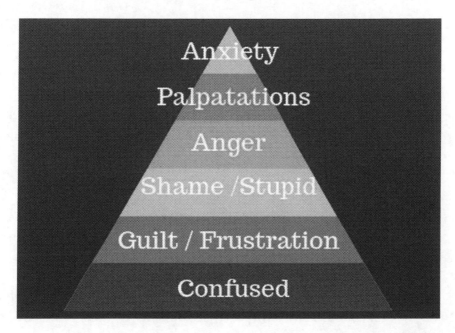

It may be that initially to combat this feeling of "Confusion" to a situation, we look around us and see that everyone else "Gets" (understands) what's going on and we don't.

This may result in feeling "Stupid" or ashamed that we don't understand what we should have done. We then assess the situation and see what we can do about it. We may realise we need to "GET that thing" that everyone else has, so we don't look out of place.

Think of musical chairs... the music stops... child 1 hasn't got a chair. They feel stupid and push child 2 off their chair and sit on it so they feel better. Child 1 then sees the impact their reaction has on everyone around them and then feels "Guilty" for pushing child 2 off their chair, plus "Stupid/ashamed" for doing it. Then "Confusion" kicks in because they don't really know what else to do! See how the layers' progress?

So, unless we have the correct skills to deal with each layer or the base layer they build and build and build, until we are a magnificent temple of negative layer on top of negative layer. Sadly, over time we may not even realise it's a problem because it's been with us for so long. "It's just who I am"! Sound familiar?

And that's just right, it's exactly who we are and we should be proud of each and every memory that has brought us to this point.

However, we now have a choice, as we are not ignorant anymore to these layers within us. We become more and more aware as we go through life and possibly as you read this, of our patterns of behaviour and how it has impacted on our life and those "OMG not again" moments.

YO-YOING TRIGGERS

If overtime (and this could be decades), we do not learn how to release these triggers effectively, then our energy system will start to overload or become blocked. This may result in mental or physical health problems. Problems such as anxiety, bi-polar, a sore throat, poorly tummy, binge eating or drinking too much, as each layer develops its own tactic of defence, using all our senses.

It's hardly surprising then, that we, (just like I did), Yo-Yo between patterns of behaviour, the good and the bad. Even though, we've worked out what we should logically do, we can't sustain keeping it at bay because our energy system is still trying to stop us from having that initial emotional rush.

Letting go of each trigger (emotion) to the behaviour is easier the younger we are, **if**, we know how to do it. It takes more time and patience the older we get, as we have developed so many behaviours to our triggers. Our energy system is a wonderful, wonderful gift for us all and we can only work properly with it when we know how.

So, this book has been created to help you make those connections, as logically as possible so you can start to use Energy Therapy techniques such as Tapping to create new patterns of behaviour, which suit you moving forward, as you are now, rather than as you were then; be that a child, or you yesterday, or even a minute ago.

Tapping is just one type of Energy Therapy but it lends itself perfectly to the explanations and charts in this book. Reiki practitioners, Yogis and all therapists, as well as individuals and families will find these charts just as fascinating to use with their clients and each other as I did. Energy Therapy is infinite and interchangeable and if you are ever told there is only one way of doing something please investigate further, as the joy of energy is that it never ends, just keeps transforming into something else.

What does that mean?

Albert Einstein's equation E=MC2 is one of the most important discoveries in the law of Science. (The energy content of a body, is equal to the mass of the body, times the speed of light squared).

Light travels at the highest speed we can quantify with vibrational sources called frequencies. If we travelled at the speed of light around the earth, we would travel around it 7.5 times in just 1 second. We wouldn't be able to watch that journey with our naked eye as the vibrational frequency is too high (too fast) for humans.

However, as the equation says, light is in all matter and energy is in all light and matter. If this is the Law of Physics then everything we see and touch and hear is vibration, just at different frequencies. Thus, so is everything we don't, see, hear or touch. It is just on a vibrational level we humans are not tuned into.

So, if we are vibration in a physical form as humans, then it makes sense that to fix any problems in our human form, we adjust the vibrational frequency accordingly, to make ourselves heal emotionally and physically. This is how Energy Therapy works.

Medical Science is slowly, very slowly starting to move more in this direction and the effects, not surprisingly, are highly effective. Dr Bruce Lipton, Author of Biology of Belief, Wisdom of Your Cells and Spontaneous Evolution, and one of the Top Stem Cell Consultants & Lecturers in the world left his Research position in 1985 after his studies made him realise traditional methods of medicine were out of date. "New science" as Energy Therapy is being called, (even though its origins are timeless since mankind has been around), is shattering old medical myths and is now able to document how energy based treatments are so highly effective.

Science is showing that Energy is infinite and constantly transforming to different vibrational frequencies, biologically, chemically, physiologically and at the speed of your thoughts. This is why the Law of Attraction and the book "The Secret" are so popular. Keeping your senses and thoughts focused and clear on what you want in life, is what spirals us to success, or stagnation.

So experiment, explore and keep moving forward, but most of all enjoy getting to know yourself and those you care about on this most beautiful and precious of journeys.

Learning to Spiral from the inside out is the start of our journey now. It takes just 5 simple Steps.

Enjoy....

STEP 1 - Awaken

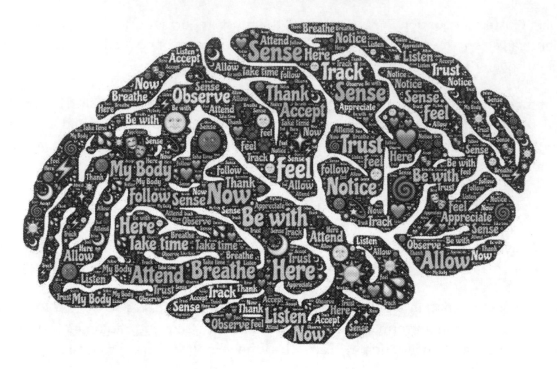

Awaken to what?

First Step: Acknowledging any sensory disruption mentally or physically in your system that doesn't feel right. ie: Being aware that something is causing a reaction in you and then admitting **really truthfully** to yourself if it's causing a problem or not.

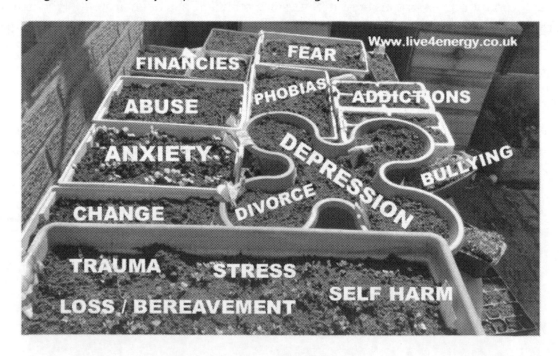

Being able to recognise your or someone else's reaction and catch yourself before you respond to it or shortly after you've responded to it is a challenge. This is often referred to as being Mindful. If you could sit and observe your reactions and behaviour from a distance i.e. imagine watching yourself in a movie when you're in a highly charged experience what would you observe using all your senses?

You can do this after an event and play out the sequence on the movie screen in front of you without letting yourself get emotional involved as your play it out, just the facts as to what happened. Tune in however, to how did you feel; where did you feel it; what did you see, hear, touch, smell and react to? Why did you do that?

Second Step:

Once you've recognised your feelings to your behaviour, are they serving you well, right now? Is it helping you move forward in life? Are you giving power to your emotion? If so, is this a pattern of behaviour repeating itself in a good way? Be aware: i.e.: Guilt, shame and embarrassment are core feelings which feed anger, frustration, jealousy and longing. These in turn may feed violence or other inappropriate acts towards each other.

So first of all we need to **AWAKEN** our senses and learn to listen, observe, feel, taste and experience ourselves on a new level.

"Ie: Be aware if work becomes a problem; relationships are suffering, are you struggling to get up in the morning, as you haven't slept well with all that "stuff" in your head. Your health may start to suffer; lack of energy; not eating properly; struggling to fit it all in; everyone wants more and more of you; you're exhausted; you're brains foggy; that cough keeps coming back and you just can't shake it off the same... and on and on."

You probably know your signals already. You've just not had the time to really take notice, so you've taken the next quick fix to get you through that little bit longer.

Chocolate, alcohol, caffeine, medication... Sound familiar?

Before I started to awaken properly, my communication over decades had gradually gone on a downwards spiral.

"From the age of 19-40 (minus 4 years to care for my 3 boys (under 6) when I found myself minus my partner – **STAGE 1** of major downward Spiral), I was mainly surrounded by engaged and inspiring individuals whose main aim in life was to think out of the box and create something new and exciting for millions of people. I worked at Granada Television which became ITV Studios and it was my working family for nearly 20 years. Intense working relationships were formed in each Department and Production I worked in, some just for 3 or

6 months, as we tirelessly put together these works of art. In fact, so engaged and inspired were the Writers, Executive Producers, Producers, Directors, Cast, Crew and office staff that the production "The Street" won a BAFTA and EMMY during it's time. Even though I wasn't an instrumental part of this team, I was involved, along with the excitement and emotions throughout the process, as I cried reading the initial scripts from conception to completion; then filming, editing and finally transmission came and went.

Suddenly this bubble burst too and ITV moved the Drama Department from Manchester to London and we were all redundant. **Stage 2** of my downward spiral, but I didn't have time to delve too deeply into my emotions, I had to keep us afloat and get another job.

I secured a great contract working for a hub of 7 schools organising out of school activities for the cluster and their families. I loved this role and my background served me well in setting up and scheduling 2 years' worth of activities for all involved. It also opened up a deeper awareness of how families need support to communication and engage together on other levels, such as fun and laughter away from the grind of everyday life. Children today especially Teens have the whole world of information at their fingertips and their sensitive systems cannot make sense of what is going on in the world. They are suffering from a complete sensory overload from all areas; home, school and online. Learning to take fun time out for the whole family is so important.

Stage 3 spiral came after this contract and a significant relationship in my life both ended at roughly the same time. I was struggling to have any confidence in myself to move forward from a work perspective. I was just about holding it together to get the boys fed, clean clothes and off to school. My focus was foggy, I struggled to see any way forward and had lost belief in my capabilities. This time I was out of work for 6 months as I struggled to keep the boys and I, financially and emotionally above water. This pattern was getting tougher and tougher each time and I didn't know what to do to break it.

I was already reading self-help books, and watching YouTube videos and going to church with the boys, then Bible Study to further my journey of spiritual self- discovery. This led me to questions further afield and discover more about the science behind spirituality. The two combined produce an understand like we've never had before. Now you've started your own journey of discover you'll see what I mean."

I eventually sat back and asked myself a very important question about everything I was experiencing and broke it down into smaller and smaller chunks overtime:

Is it REALLY ok with me when I experience that?
If it's not... why not?

Use this page to makes Notes on this and use to start Tapping with:

EXPERIENCE Person/ Event/ Place /	IS IT OK? Y/N	WHY NOT? How is it making you feel, see, hear, taste, touch?

STEP 2 - Engage

In the process of understanding **What** you are now **AWAKE** to, communication starts to take place within yourself and possibly others.

The biggest wake up call, is do you have the COURAGE to do something about it? Being safe is a primitive instinct within us to protect us from harm. Why shake it up?

"Before I started to wake up, depression really started to seep in. I withdrew from my friends and family and I became a recluse, even struggled to apply for jobs as my uuumph had well and truly gone. I was wallowing in my own misery with no idea how to get out."

Stage 4 had set in big time (these Spiral go up and down like waves so you feel great one minute like you're moving forward then the next wave takes your feet right out from under you).

"I finally landed a job locally which fitted in with family life but other circumstances became difficult. I found myself again in a situation where my personal space was being invaded daily. Eventually, it became easier to leave, flight mode again kicked in and I moved to another local company and life couldn't have been more different. I was suddenly surrounded by boundaries everywhere I looked. Everything and everyone seemed hemmed in by rules and regulations. There was no freedom to actually move forward. The drive and inspiration had been sucked out of the place long before I encountered it and as much as I tried to make an impact on it, I realised I didn't have the will or energy left to really engage and do it.

I had sunk further into the belief system of needing to "put up and shut up" to pay the bills and didn't have the energy or courage for any further confrontation with male colleagues or men full stop. It started to seep into all my senses. The smell of despair, sneers of contempt and negativity were part of the environment that enveloped everyone who worked there, sucking the life out of everyone. It was like a contagious disease and I was seriously in danger of catching it.

I started to feel lost and trapped and watched those around me give their lives to something they saw no alternative to and certainly too much fear to do anything about. The sad thing was the most negative individuals were so young to seemingly give up and give in to it. The over 40's outwardly appeared more buoyant and resigned to their lot. The younger ones were resentful and angry, mainly I believe, at themselves, for getting trapped and too frightened to try anything else, and I could certainly relate to it. Some appeared to get a RUSH of power when they took it out on others. It perhaps eased their own emotional embarrassment and guilt for staying where they were and giving in to their environment and fear of the unknown outside world.

I had been unconsciously directing my energy to helping a young man with his inner- conflict and self-worth. I knew I could make a difference here and help guide him through his internal chaos. I could see it would be of huge value to me and him in the long run. The company conflict was bigger than me and I sat back to listen and observe as to what could be done on that score.

I knew what I was doing and yet I knew I was putting myself at risk in the environment I was in. It did not lend itself to helping others like this. It was a mechanical machine of production and egos were high.

This whole environment created chaos in my energy system with triggers going crazy, layer on layer. I started to spiral mentally and physically into despair, faster and faster each day, knowing I was in the wrong place but now too far down the spiral to have the energy to think or act effectively. I'd nearly given up and realisation hit home with a BANG, as the young mans' fight mechanism made a massive final spurt against me. I absorbed it all and understood what was at the core of the issue and chose to be more lenient than "professionally" I should have been. I was repeating pattern, after pattern, after pattern in my life, of not just taking responsibility of my own actions but taking on someone else's actions too. I took on the guilt, shame, disappointment, frustration, and confusion for us both.

A few weeks later everything suddenly just slotted into place. I knew I'd done everything I could, apart from one thing. I spent the next 10 minutes gathering things together and letting one colleague know where I was going, and walked very calmly out of the door.

The realisation when I got home that as a single mum I was responsible for a mortgage and 3 boys, sank in. I collapsed in a heap and sobbed my heart out with no idea what I was going to do to bring the money in if I didn't go back. However, that RUSH of relief when I woke the next morning was just immense, knowing just for that day I didn't have to go back into that environment; I knew without a doubt I'd made the right decision. The stress of it all had made me ill and I needed time to recover emotionally and physically. Only this time I couldn't just throw myself into looking for another job. My body and mind were making me take time out and really assess my life. I realised I had some serious work to do, but this time I was prepared to give myself time for the boys and I, to truly move forward.

I used this time wisely using Energy Therapy to clear triggers, blockages and finding new releases for each new emotion that I faced. The real test, came after numerous energy therapy sessions, in a final meeting with the owner of the Manufacturing company, at an internal tribunal. We put to bed all the issues I raised in my complaint letter when I walked out. I managed to face it without fear; calmly, concisely, focused and effectively and most importantly with complete integrity. The result for me, was knowing I had finally faced the fear of confrontation with a male authority figure in a work environment, especially when I felt I had everything to lose.

Finally, I had made my voice matter, in a manner that I was proud of. I had finally found my courage!

Letting go of all the emotions from the past events didn't leave me as vulnerable as I feared it would. In fact, it empowered me to be strong and courageous and calm from a really deep place within. The words, the humour, the listening skills and response I was able to give, even surprised me. I had tuned into the deepest part of me and was being led from a place of total peace and acceptance. Nothing he said fazed me.

Finally, the company were facing up to complaints for bullying in the workplace. I chose to not take legal proceeding but made sure that every meeting was recorded and registered with the correct procedures, so they had a blue print to work with for the future. I had been prevented from performing as I would have liked and I wanted to give something of value to the company as a parting gift. So, this was my gift. So, This was my gift to them, and I say gift because that's how I chose to see it and present it.

The second result was an added bonus. The young man who I had been emotionally mentoring, I asked to see before I left, and before I could speak he thanked me for all the advice I had given him and told me he had finally been able to come out and tell everyone his story (not for me to share I'm afraid). Understanding how huge this was for him, I was able to let go of the fact he didn't apologise for his actions leading up to me leaving. Right then that didn't matter. I knew that, plus more, would be part of his journey to come.

The freedom I felt from this experience was immense. This was one of the most empowering moments I had experienced to that day, and may I say when you start to be really true to yourself, and you clear the old emotional triggers, these moments get better and more beautiful and joyful than you have ever felt before. They smash the negative moments of gaining control completely out of the ball park."

As I continued training as an Energy Therapist, I have worked tirelessly with my clients to ensure they understand they can "Bridge The Gap" to unleash their true values and recover quicker and quicker each time they have a major challenge in their life.

My tools for Energy Therapy are EFT (Emotional Freedom Technique) which helped me shift blockages physically and emotionally and gave me a logical explanation to go with each shift. This logical perception of Energy Therapy is now what I am passing onto my clients and readers.

I am a Reiki Master and hold weekly sessions including Meditation which has helped my clients and I have clarity and peace in moving forward. Feeling safe and greater clarity gives you such Freedom.

As a Master NLP (Neuro Linguistic Programming) Practitioner this assisted with reframing and releasing blockages/triggers during hypnotic conversation or hypnosis, ie: in a relaxed to deeply relaxed state.

I have found that combining the therapies works wonderfully too. That's the beauty of Energy Therapy its transformation on a vibrational level is infinite.

All of these, are tools which everyone can access and enable, to massively impact on Your Positive Mental Health, which in turn feeds your physical health.

The attached charts have been created to give a logical guide to our energy system and how to begin communication with it. They are a "guide" as these emotions and symptoms may also be present in other areas. However, it gives you and others, a way of understanding emotions and yo-yoing behaviour, and allows compassion to flow towards others as we begin to understand more fully, these connections emotionally and physically.

Imagine gaining a real understanding that Dad/Uncle has felt lost, alone and abandoned, not because he's told us about it but the yawning, excessive sweating, watering eyes or coughing being released as you work through the charts together, is understanding enough. These releases may allow him to talk about it later.

Teens start to make the connection that yawning or coughing, and giggling may be a release from the area we are working on. Siblings and mums too. The connection it gives back to that family to communicate on a sensory level is breathtakingly beautiful.

Connections begin to happen when those headaches come on again and there's been stress at school or work. Individuals know where to look on the chart and start the process of self-healing themselves before picking up the phone to the doctors.

Beautiful communication begins to happen in your family previously unnoticed before.

How Does This Work?

The information stored in our energy system has various systems that work together. Scientifically what happens is that as the vibrational frequencies in our system start to move there is a chemical reaction.

This reaction creates a transformation, which flows through our Meridian system, which are electrical pulses processing through our body like a river. Each Meridian has a starting point and end point some beginning or ending at the end of fingers and toes. Most listed here run through main internal organs in your body which is why they are called Heart Meridian / Small intestine Meridian, etc.

When a Meridian is vibrated (Tapped on) transformations happen at a cellular level as the vibrational force of our pulses move our cells together, faster or slower; colliding or not colliding; becoming diseased or replenishing new healthy cells, depending on our state of being, negative or positive. It becomes a cycle, a spiral, a pattern of emotion, feeding behaviour, feeding emotion, feeding behaviour, feeding our physical health, feeding emotion, etc.

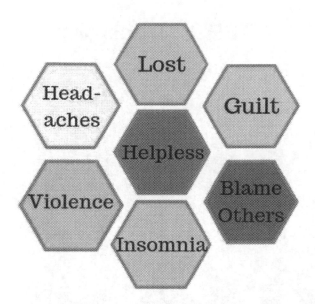

Thus, as our thoughts/feelings/attitudes of behaviour are all vibration they have a massive impact on how our energy levels and possible disease (diabetes, cancer, obesity, etc) and mental health (Bi-polar, stress, anger, love, compassion) effect our physical body.

We will look at this further in the latter section of the book within the charts and an explanation on Meridians.

STEP 3 - Transform

What action can you take?

As we have now established we have an energy system which uses all our senses. Action may be taken on the sensory area which is on high alert or you wish to work on.

Various Energy Therapies for this are listed below:

Acupressure

Acupuncture

Aromatherapy

Ayurvedic Medicine

Chiropractic

EFT (Emotional Freedom Technique)

Energy Medicine

Hypnosis

Meditation

NLP (Neuro-Linguistic Programme)

Reiki

QiGong

Shiatsu

Yoga

Chinese Medicine

Tapping

Numerology

Music Therapy

Homeopathy

Nutrition Plus many, many, more........

Some of these you will need Practitioner help with and some you will be able to start on your own by reading books, the internet and YouTube etc. If there is a deep issue such as abuse, bipolar or serious physical ailment, or your working with children, then having an Energy Therapist work with you is recommended.

With each new Energy Therapy you try, it is important to realise that our energy system will need time to Wake Up to this new communication process. Think on the basis that our energy system has been in a very deep sleep for a very long time and waking it up gently with a little and often is usually the best way to approach this new style of living.

Learning to Engage with each new sense that Awakens allows you to clear any issues blocked there. Your energy system is very good at showing you what it is ready to release. This is the start of peeling off the layers of each trigger and the more we immerse ourselves into the new practice then the more responsive our whole energy system will become.

Please remember all of this work is a lifetime process. We are never completely healed because we've had one session of Energy Therapy such as Reiki or Tapping. We pick up new triggers every day to be released.

The more open you are to working with your own energy system the quicker and easier we start to move up the spiral positively and start to **let go** of old patterns.

LETTING GO

Letting Go what does this mean? If we think of every emotion we have it is attached, always attached to something; an event, person, place etc. If each emotion attached to that past event; smile, noise, taste, angry face, was on a movie screen, imagine you are able to switch channels inside our head to each new emotion. How would you like to deal with that event as you, right now, in this moment, on that movie screen? Would you change anything? If the answer is yes, then perhaps releasing old emotions would help that process.

Being able to release the old emotions gives us more space inside us which allows us to deal with the new experiences in a manner we prefer.

Yes, I know it sounds simple. But to do it in the heat of the moment, "that moment" can be very difficult. This is where Energy Therapy comes in.

But let's continue with Letting Go first. It is one of the largest lessons we learn in life and it is certainly not easy. We start the process and as we manage to move forward our Fight, Flight or Freeze (Triple Warmer Meridian) mechanism kicks back in and checks that this is what we really want to do.

Our energy system is much more intelligent than our logical brain and recognises similar signals to the old ones. SO it may say "Whoah! Hang on!! Let me check you really want this! I've protected you your whole life and we've never done this before. Let me just give you that poorly tummy again just to make sure". The dodgy tummy will take impact if you haven't been clearing out that tiredness; or trying to fit in too much of your stuff and everyone else's stuff too; binge watching box sets, becoming an App addict or on social media, drinking too much; eating the wrong things, etc.

If you imagine yourself as a large sponge that has been soaked in a bucket of water, when you're lifted out you leak everywhere with excess water. That's exactly how our mind & body works. If we soak up too many emotional experiences or overload our body with excess food and drink, there will be a trigger to overload.

There is a way to control the triggers (squeeze your sponge) and that is to be in control of what you release before you become too saturated and it reaches a critical level.

SO HOW DO WE DO IT?

As the saying goes "There's a season, a reason and a lifetime" and this applies to everything in our life. Work, relationships, friends, money, meetings, animals, houses, holidays, nature and more.

The people who stay in our lives the longest are usually our roots and yet we don't always know if they're the roots until our time here is nearly over.

The people that stay for decades or a few years may be our branches and the leaves may be those who stay for a season or two. Some may just be for a reason and pass through briefly in a moment, an hour, a day. I'm sure we all have a memory of someone who impacted our lives with just a look, a smile, an accidental touch, a line from a video, music track, book that resonated with us still today. Each one will have been there for a lesson we needed to learn, either in that moment, or in the time we take to digest it and absorb it.

The hard part is learning to decipher who may be sticking around and who isn't and then, perhaps Not leap into marrying the person who was meant for a season.

Letting go emotionally of attachments we make, and recognising and learning how to do this is a skill, and it is a skill. It is something we can all learn to do, and with love and compassion too.

Learning to be grateful for that seasonal time, enjoy that time, relish that time, say thank you and let them walk away freely with your love and blessing, is our lesson. Sometimes we don't do this because we try to hold onto very tightly, frightened of what will happen if they leave us to cope alone. Maybe they gave us such an important lesson very early on and we were so grateful for it we want their experience and knowledge to last even longer in our life.

The lesson is to awaken to the experience we've been given, acknowledge it and engage in doing something to make it part of our life in our own way. Then, if they are meant to come back into our life, they will, in their own time.

So How Do We tell The Difference?

It's tough!! And sometimes we get it wrong. Plus, its hurts when we have to let people go, especially if we want them and they don't want us anymore. But change will happen with or without you. It always has, and will continue long after we are gone. Try to look at time as infinite. It is energy just as we are, so who knows when we'll meet again and where.

Being flexible in your approach and yet having boundaries which reflect your values is vitally important.

"When I found myself alone with 3 boys under the age of 6, my whole world crumbled and I only managed to physically move myself out of bed for the sake of the boys. Each day I managed to do that I somehow gathered some momentum and within a 6 month period, I'd found a job, looked after the boys, walked the dog, ran the home, sorted the finances, and endeavoured to be physically and mentally strong enough to keep doing it.

And, thankfully, along the way we meet people who help us through. I met a lovely lady who became one of my closest friends during this time and our friendship was never dull. We seemed to go through mammoth changes each week involving work, men, children, family and friends. It was filled with hysterical belly laughs, tears and soul searching conversations and I felt blessed that we had this beautiful friendship.

What I had not envisaged was that the life changing experiences I was having would have such a detrimental effect on my friend.

Although I could cope with the larger than life personalities popping in and out of my life and could let them go once they had moved on. I had not taken into consideration if my friend could cope with my offloading chatter about what was happening, on top of her own emotional rollercoaster life.

In short, my "Letting go" wasn't the right kind of letting go. I dumped it all on one person rather than spreading the load of my emotional, crazy life and expected that person to even enjoy the ride with me. Only over time, for her it wasn't a ride of enjoyment, it was of worry and concern because she cared and she could see some outcomes before I was even willing to glimpse at what they may be. But that was my journey and lessons I had to take on board.

I learnt the hard way. As usual, I had to experience it for myself.

If I had spread the load, perhaps talking with other friends or family; meditating; using EFT (Tapping); Reiki, even writing down a pros and cons list it may have helped to prevent what happened.

She is a very spiritual lady and laughingly always tried to keep me as grounded as possible, fearing I'd fly away with all the ideas I had in my head and shared with everyone I could.

Eventually, when I'd disappointed her once to many with my decision making I believe she lost respect for me. Bless her, she stayed with me right up until she could see I was at an even keel in life emotionally, then she quietly slipped away and disappeared into the background and out of my life. It hurt so much that I'd hurt someone I cared about so much, that she had to walk away from me to feel better.

This was another downward spiral.

I did not want the people I cared about to keep walking away from me, so they felt better. I didn't want to be the energy vampire I believe I must have become, using their energy field to feed my own instead of fuelling and sustaining myself.

Sometime later, I went on a training day for EFT and I was being worked on as the client. We had tapped through clearing various emotions and I now had a vision of lots of balloons (like the ones in the film "Up" that took his house "Up") and the practitioner asked me what I wanted to do with these balloons. I tuned into my senses and I said I believe they wanted to be free. I was asked how would I free them and I said cut them free as they wanted to fly. So we cut them free.

After I had let them go I had a heart stopping moment when I realised what the balloons were connected to. They were the metaphor my friend had used to keep reeling me back in with when she thought I should be more grounded. It was a sad but enlightening moment for me rolled into one. I realised I had let us both go from our ties to each other and that saddened me very much until I realised I'd needed to let her go so that we could both fly on with our journeys.

(It also made me realise that she had always talked about reeling the kite back in (me) and I had altered the image as she had been originally talking, to one that I preferred, which were balloons. Please note that what someone tells us and what we perceive will not always align. We are masters of our own imagination so be aware that what you tune into during a conversation is Your interpretation and no one else's). Always good to be aware for future discussions on what was said and what was interpreted.

Ultimately, my friend had needed to protect herself from my full on need for an energy fix on life, and she couldn't see my boundaries to work with. My friend had been developing her own boundaries/values and chose to leave my chaos behind, and I don't blame her. It wasn't for her, and it must have drained her physically and mentally, which on top of her own life was too much. It turned out the people I was attracting were a lesson I needed but only for a season or two. I'd just not let go soon enough.

My belief system was such that, once a friend always a friend, and I'd assumed she would be a root to my tree as I would have been hers, but the branch broke under the fruit with which it was laden. The fruit which she provided for me on a season by season and year by year account with her knowledge, wisdom and sharing and when the bough broke it was with the weight of my life choices."

So, share the laughter and tears my friends, and keep your roots if they mean that much to you. Work on "Yourself" and Bridge The Gap of emotions from the past and behaviours which are not serving you right now. Remember, the people you care about need nourishing and caring for at a very deep level too and clearing yourself out allows them to escape your emotional overloading.

Working on yourself is a constant life journey, releasing sooner rather than later helps you focus so much more clearly ahead on your true path.

If, however, it's a lesson you need to learn as I did. Acknowledge that it happened. Engage to make the necessary changes to nourish yourself, because if you've fed and nourished yourself at the core, then you have something truly worthwhile and of value to nourish others with.

WHAT ARE THE DIFFERENCES OF ENERGY THERAPY?

Now we have established that we are all vibrating at different frequencies, and to self- heal we need to adjust our vibrational frequencies to remove negative blockages in our system.

How may we do this?

We may do this by tapping, holding, listening, thinking, talking, looking, moving our bodies and mind to a more specific vibrational frequency. Technically this is where you may start to do your own deeper research as this area is VAST. I have included a reading/audiobook material list at the back of the book to help start you off.

A brief guide follows:

EFT (Emotional Freedom Technique) was created by Gary Craig in the 1980's using the Chinese art of Medicine and Meridians plus the language of NLP (Neuro Linguistic Programming) to reframe your thoughts. He fined tuned it into the wonderful Energy Therapy it is today. He discovered that you do not have to use needles like in acupuncture or all the meridian points to clear yourself of blockages for Emotional Freedom Technique to be effective. Crossing your energy meridians with Tapping is just as effective.

Richard Bandler, and John Grindor are the creators of NLP (Neuro Linguistic Programming) a method to understand and change people behaviour patterns using hypnotic language.

Donna Eden (Founder of Energy Medicine) discovered that you do not even have to touch yourself to move the energy around your meridian system. You can guide it with your thoughts or hands.

Reiki healing can be a hands off, hands on and even sent as distance healing therapy for effective results. It is still moving and working with your energy system vibrating at a very high level which most of us cannot see or hear.

How do these methods work?

They work by the practitioner tuning into your unique energy vibrational system and helping you alter the frequency with the techniques they are trained in to benefit you. The more consistently you use these techniques in your life the more your energy system keeps the techniques/frequencies in place. We are constantly changing with new experiences in life every day so we just need to keep on top of each new frequency change.

Once you start to use the charts attached and tune into your own energy system you will start to make connections with your own emotional and physical self. Over time you will find your own way of working for small clearances. Larger clearances are always advised to work through with a Practitioner or with someone you trust.

The Tap Around The Clock charts take a step back from Gary Craig's EFT use. They connect each tapping point with a time, a meridian and an emotional or physical problem to bring some logic to individuals just starting their energy therapy journey or therapy business.

Once seen and then used as in the chart, it all seems rather simple, so to be perfectly honest when you first start Tapping you may feel rather "silly"! And guess what?

That's always the first thing I recommend you start to tap out.

> *"So even though I feel really silly tapping all over my face and hands right now. I accept that I do, because I do. And I accept me anyway"* Repeat 3 times with short circuit at end. See Methods.....

When you've done this you can start on any of the methods at the back of this book.

Meridians How They Work

Touch, sight, smell, taste, hearing & feeling are all senses that contain blockages in our energy system (ie blocked frequencies). The internal Meridian clock takes note of all these senses, and highlights when particular organs/areas of our body are working at their optimum time or weakest times in relation to the Meridian/GMT clock. For example, our Spleen Meridian works at its optimal level between 9-11am, and opposite this is our Triple Warmer meridian which is at is weakest during this time. The Triple Warmer works best between 9-11PM and therefore the spleen is at is weakest then. They are the Ying and Yang to each other and need nourishing and balancing to work effectively or one will hold more energy than the other.

If we are worrying and anxious between 9-11pm, it is usually because our Spleen meridian has not been fed enough energy or is blocked. So our Triple Warmer Meridian may be taking the Spleen's power away, getting stronger and stronger. This means our fight, flight and freeze mechanisms may be pumping at full speed ahead.

Anxiety and fear will be at their highest here if this is the case.

It's hardly surprising so many people can't get to sleep when they are worrying about everything that happened to them in life during 9pm – 11pm at night.

To calm this down we need to feed our spleen more energy, and release blockages from here and the Triple Warmer Meridian, so the flow of our internal Meridian clock is healthier. We can do this by tapping on each point and asking to release emotions/physical pain blocked in each area, or giving positive emotions a boost from the positive chart.

For example, a significant number of heart attacks happen during SPLEEN (9-11am) time as the spleen is underworked/blocked and cannot feed the heart, not necessarily because there is a heart "problem" as such.

All our senses are meant to flow freely like a waterfall. If our whole energy system flows freely we are emotionally, physically and spiritually healthier.

At this point you may wish to proceed straight to work on the Charts. Feel free to do so.

Once you have started work on your meridian system the following will start to happen.

STEP 4 - Inspire

Inspiration comes from that divine place, your spirit (energy system) so it is a sensation that is immediately filled with JOY when you have that RUSH of Inspiration.

How can others not be intrigued as to where this new found JOY has come from as it pours out of your whole being?

I have found that the JOY of sharing this journey of Awakening, Engaging and Transformation becomes infectious, vibrant and contagiously fun.

I have been compelled to share it with as many families as possible so they can survive the challenges of life with effective skills and language tools than I didn't have when I found myself a single mum.

"My adjustment from feeling secure and happy as a family unit changed to feeling abandoned, unloved and frightened for the future. With 3 boys under 6, no job and alone this was my main downward spiral for the next 10 years.

Logically I had life worked out as to why it happened and what I needed to do but I yo-yoed so much trying to rectify it, I damaged me and my boys in the process. I didn't have the resilience from the heartbreak and exhaustion, to see clearly or function clearly. Everything became a battle, especially at home.

Heartbreakingly, I projected a lot of my guilt, shame, worry and fear onto my boys by my actions of an overtired, frustrated, overly anxious, confused, doubting, financial worrying, emotionally drained woman, and I certainly had no self-confidence left to believe in any decision I made as the right one. When I asked for help from the boys' dad he was probably going through similar emotions, so it was never forthcoming.

This was probably when I felt the most lonely, abandoned and helpless.

These emotions keep us in a constant fight, flight or freeze mode until they are dealt with. As some of you may understand from your own experiences this is a time of high anxiety, stress, guilt and feeling generally unsafe. How can we make the best decisions when we are on constant high alert. You switch constantly between feeling everything's a threat or a lifeline.

Being a parent is the most difficult job in the world so making the decision to back off or plough straight in can only be done with the tools we have at the time.

My mum was a wonderful parent and innocently left me to my own devices as a teenager, trusting me to do the right thing.

How does a child or anyone know what is the right thing when they start on a new adventure and they are receiving what they want, right there and then? Just like when we were babies crying to be fed, our needs are met. The signals may be slightly different once we're older. We may not be physically crying but our emotional needs still crave to be met.

If someone is giving us emotional or physical attention that we feel we need right there and then and that need is being met, the "Confusion" will kick in if it goes against the values we have been taught along the way. This is where we start the process of real self-responsibility.

What do I mean about the values we set our self?

"As a teenager I played the Flugel Horn and was in the school brass band. An activity I'd started to take very seriously in my final year at school, after a previous school performance at the Royal Albert Hall had inspired me to be the best I could be in my final year there.

I spent every day of the summer 6 week holiday practicing my instrument determined to improve, and the change was pretty impressive. It went noticed and I was suitably praised and fawned over by my music teacher who elevated me to soloist position within the band pretty much Immediately. I'd worked so hard for this moment and my heart ached with pride and love for the joy it brought.

I had found my passion and nothing was going to get in my way. I attended every band practice, every concert, every lesson, every band holiday and every other band member was the same. We idolised our Band Leader and would have run over hot coals for the man who inspired us all to achieve the status of Best School Band in Britain.

Rachel Earing

Our final school concert was an emotional affair. The school had 7 bands and each band played in the concert with the finale played out by the School Band due to disband and move on after this final year together. All the families and friends were there for each band of which there were possible 35+ students in each one. Needless to say the room was heaving, in great spirits and the atmosphere was amazing.

Our final time had come and **my** final time of standing in front of teachers, families and friends to play my solo. My piece was the famous Barbra Streisand "Send In The Clowns" and I was nervous as I stood to take the stage. Something felt different tonight and I couldn't put my finger on it.

I stood and faced the audience, my mother and friends eagerly waiting in the middle for it to begin. Our Band Master smiled his smile and counted us in....

I started beautifully and off I began. The more I played, the more a strange feeling started to seep up through my body into my chest and I couldn't work out what it was. I was glad for the interlude where I could take a breath and sort myself out.

The feeling grew rather than subsided and as I prepared to join back in for my big finale, I looked at our Conductor and He gave me that look........ that look which said.... That's my girl..... I'm so proud of you..... This is your moment.

This is the man that inspired me to be the best I could be. I wanted to impress him, thrill him, let him see that I could achieve. I wanted to feel that feeling of "I'm special". I idolised this man. I wanted to shine and be the light for others to give it a go... take action, do something every day ...... and things change ......musically and.....psychologically.

It was nearly time for me to join back in. The bands interlude has finishing and....

I suddenly see all those girls in the band as I look round, only now they have clown faces laughing at me as they play, nearly ready for me to join in.....

I look at our conductor..... He has the biggest Clown face and costume on. He's laughing hysterically at me waving his baton for me to play...... I know then.... I'll never tell anybody what went on..... ever

I'm too stupid.... I'm the Clown..... He's the clown. We're all the clowns!

I decide there and then with that one look....... He's having no more of me, not a note

.... Not a tear.... nothing.

I sit down and look ahead as the band struggle to carry on without me. They think I've bottled it.

I don't care.... right there and then, I don't care what they think. I deserve this shame.

I deserve this punishment of 400 family and friends being there to witness my disgrace.

Because I am a disgrace..... a stupid, stupid girl who should have know.... like they did.....I wasn't special...

I wasn't important.... I wasn't attractive.... I was just a stupid Clown. ....letting everyone there, down; letting my band members down...... to make it KNOWN to him! It was OVER and never again would he have any part of me. He knew........ as I glared at him when he tried to get me to carry on.

He knew...... as I shook my head at the principal cornet player who tried to rescue my solo.

He knew...... as he stopped the band from finishing the piece without me.....

He knew...... right then in that moment, just as I did, it was over. He would never again be able to manipulate me into his world of pretty words and tantalising touches. He would never again, touch my neck, my thigh, my lips........

In that moment I took back my power ...... even if I was a Clown.

I sat in that room, in front of all those parents, family and friends I'd shared my teenage years with and took the emptiness of that moment and became true to me for the first time in my teenage life.

I let down others to stand in my own inner moment of power and truth and be at peace with it.

What I didn't understand in that moment is the damage that FREEZE effect would have on the rest of my life......

You see I held onto that shame, guilt, disappointment and lack of respect for myself for 30 years before I told another soul what that night was really about. The night that reaffirmed all my feelings, as I sat in the classroom on my own after the performance, watching everyone else go back to their parents have a drink, laugh and chat. As alone I sat and took in the enormity of what I had done that evening. And alone, I stayed and waited and perhaps hoped, someone, anyone, would ask me what had happened and why, yet knowing I'd never tell."

What do you value?

So life went on and during the following 30 years, I managed to react pretty much to form from that one incident. You see the freeze mechanism is one of the most dangerous protection modes we have along with flight and fight. It's a hidden cause, a cause that all that RUSH of emotions in those 3 minutes, becomes trapped like an ice berg in your system. It can become so trapped in that trauma moment it causes you to forget where it came from, you hide from it any which way you can because you do not want to face those emotions again. You will lie and cheat and blame others to take the focus away from you, over and over again until you face it and deal with it and vibrate it out of your system.

The last 30 years my freeze mechanism resulted in me self-sabotaging my marriage; work situations; relationships; friendships and my mental health. Why, because not acknowledging what had happened in those teenage years led me to lie to myself or blame others, or hide and deny anything that challenged those feelings coming forward again. Thus, I lost the ability to persevere with anything I became passionate about as I didn't have the skills to challenge future perpetrators in my life especially male authoritative figures (and when I say authoritative that could have been within my professional, physically, emotionally or financial life) wherever I allowed them to have a position of power over me.

Those old emotions had frozen in my system as a self defence mechanism for my future passions and the shame, guilt, embarrassment and confusion soon made me believe I wasn't worthy enough to have that end result of a dream marriage, fabulous career or financial rewards.

That was until now, and the new musical instrument I am learning to play, which will take a lifetime and more to master. A passion I have for tuning in my new strings to play the music I always wanted and then to help others learn how to do the same."

Energy Therapy is my new musical instrument and it motivated me to clear these old stuck emotions so I didn't let myself, my clients or my family down by not facing my own demons. It also enables a true understanding of what my clients face on their journey to the other side – emotional freedom!

I used Tapping to clear these emotions stuck like glue to my strings and my perpetrators of 30+ years which released this self-sabotaging behaviour out of my life.

So what did I get out of that particular relationship that the 15 year old me needed?

I received the attention that a teenager turning into a young woman was being acknowledged and appreciated from someone I idolised and admired. He wasn't just one of the guys from school. He was THE guy from school, older, wiser, knowledgeable, interesting, and knew just what to say and do to tune into me. I had attention for my talents and my emotional and physical self. I got what I longed for and the romantic part of me believed this rush of intense emotion was worthy of being a root to my tree....

He, this inspirational man that everyone admired so much, wanted ME, so I must be special.

But I wasn't, I was the Clown, but I couldn't see that then. I knew I was running a high risk, I knew it was against all school rules and I knew he was married and I knew in the deepest parts of me it was wrong but that part of me that whispered "this is wrong, get out", wasn't loud enough and didn't feed me the RUSH of emotion that he did.

I didn't know then, that that whisper that comes to you in those quiet moment or busy moments, is actually the only part of us we should be listening to. The clue to our true answer is always in the whisper.

I was innocent and didn't have the life experience to know how to handle it nor the confidence to say no. He was the adult and I had been taught to do as I was told especially from adults. Respect was a big thing in our house as I was growing up, especially with male figures. You did as you were told.

Thus, I didn't have the skills to see through, deal with, or the self-belief to know, I was so much more than what was on offer.

Being told you are a victim in those sort of situations doesn't make you feel any more empowered either, as at the time, you never felt like a victim. You felt special and cared for in a way no one else has ever made you feel. It is only when you have detached yourself and faced the emotions attached to the events can you clearly look back and see it for what it was. You suddenly see the damage it has done to your life over the years. Especially, if it has taken you 30 years to face it.

That gap, which held all that misplaced loyalty, held repeating patterns of behaviour, after repeating pattern of behaviour, just a different face; a different place; different story until I finally learnt to face myself and give myself a higher value which included boundaries of self-care and confidence.

Bridging the gap and learning to communicate within yourself, allows the bridge to the outside world to appear. Once you've learnt the skill of communication within you, you're ready to cross the bridge and join your missing pieces together.

I helped to Bridge this gap through EFT and Tania A Prince's, Mindfulness Based Inner Repatterning, by clearing different aspects of this event.

I felt safe using these methods because at no time did I need to mention details of what had happened. It was worked through on a treasure hunt with my physical emotions/symptoms through the body, metaphors (on this occasion "Dementors" from Harry Potter), colours and shapes. I felt safe, even though I cried, lost my voice and felt like a ball was stuck at the back of my throat.

As this all started to clear blockages from my system, the next round of tapping was intoxicatingly freeing. I was shattered, yet not exhausted. I was relaxed in a way I don't remember feeling before. It was a peaceful feeling. A oneness with such underlying tones of joy and happiness, I felt truly free. It was a very powerful experience.

The true value this freedom gives your life, impacts so positively on your confidence, self-esteem, motivation, clarity, focus and so much more."

As you start to work through your own issues, this new free you will undoubtedly then want to help others thrive. You see once you've started your own Treasure Hunt within, you can't help but want to inspire others to do the same, by sharing your knowledge and experiences of how this works.

You may also, start to notice more synchronicity in your life, as people and events start to arrive in your life at just the right time to further your development.

You may find social media groups may develop with a more focused and true purpose.

One to one meetings may become more meaningful and deep in their connection.

Group gatherings may have a feeling of intensity and excitement which only the truly inspired can generate such powerful energy from.

Family life and relationships may take on new deeper meaning and resonance, or you may find yourself free from old relationship restraints.

Once we've reached this stage we are as a collective body moving to work together more, and become sustainable for the future. We want others to join us and become as evolved emotionally and physically as we are and be able to recover from the pain and heartache quicker and faster each time. To find the joy inside the pain.

Work life balance becomes easier, eating habits become easier to fulfil, habits and patterns that were previously holding us back start to disappear.

Inspiration drives us forward as one, and with one purpose - to evolve into our true destiny

My Message from these experiences:

Persevere with Passion to Free Yourself from Self-Sabotage!

What is your destiny?

STEP 5 - Sustain

How do we Sustain this journey?

With the realisation that:

> ➢ We will **Awaken** more than once and through various spectrums (ie: EFT, Meditation, Reiki, Acupuncture, Tapping, Yoga, Hypnosis, and more) which become open to us at different times in our life journey.

> ➢ We will **Engage** with each spectrum as it opens to us more fully and with greater understanding each time. This in turn has a ripple effect on our relationships at work, home and with friends.

> ➢ We begin to **Transform** quicker and more effectively from relationships, events, accidents, environmental impacts on our lives as each upward spiral comes around. Being aware that the more open we are to this spiral the higher and more positively we will vibrate.

> ➢ We will **Inspire** more and more people around us as these changes take place within us, and unless people we care about go with us on this journey they will be out of sync with our spiral. We will begin to accept that that's ok if it's meant to be, but..... it would be so, so special, meaningful and fun if they joined us to.

> • **Most Importantly** - We realise, we cannot force these issues, people or the spiral. We cannot force others or ourselves. All of this is done through free will, and it is our own journey and inspiration (the joy in everything) driving us and them forward.

If you are able to incorporate these techniques into a daily routine, then the highs and lows of life do not make us crumble like they did before. We become resilient, compassionate and understanding, empowered and purposeful on what we wish to achieve and how to do it.

Patience and acceptance of our own journey and respect for the timing and lessons of others is our greatest learning gift. Time is infinite, but it keeps moving and flowing just like we need to do.

This resonated with me recently just before I finished this book.

"I was woken in the middle of the night and dashed to the bathroom just managing to save the bedding as I came on my menstrual cycle. Nothing unusual there.... I've been doing this a long time now and it was just the inconvenience of getting up in the night to sort myself out.

I crawled back into bed quietly, shattered, and with that back breaking ache that comes with the territory. Feeling the pain, I decided to meditate whilst lying there to ease the symptoms and just as I was drifting into the most peaceful and beautiful of places, pain free, I was brought back with my partner sliding up to me for a cuddle.

Normally I'd blend in and we'd sleep a while longer, but today was different. Anger engulfed me and I had to contain myself so he couldn't see or feel what was going on inside me. It crept up from my toes until it had taken over my entire being and I was frozen with rage. The thought "I can't even meditate without someone wanting a piece of me" flew to mind, as I'd been pulled into so many different directions recently I was obviously feeling the strain. Yet this was so much more than that. It was so intense it invaded every one of my senses and it was overwhelming me.

I became aware this wasn't really about my partner even though I'd had that initial rush of impatience. He's such a beautiful soul, and truly wouldn't hurt anyone. If he had any idea of how I was feeling he would have backed off straight away bless him. I didn't want him to feel rejected, so I stayed in this enraged state, confused and seemingly frozen in time until I could make my excuses and go downstairs to digest where this had come from.

By the time I'd washed, dressed and arrived downstairs, I wasn't just angry, I was livid! So livid, I'd actually taken the time to work out how many periods I'd had since the age of 13 and how 30 months of that was carrying 3 children and how 6 weeks after each of these was a period in itself each week. I mean who needs to know how many periods you've had (432 give or take a few) - really?

I'd worked out that on top of the physical discomfort of back pain, ovary pain, stomach cramps, migraines, dashing to the loo every hour for 24 hours when it's at its worst, changing clothes, bedding etc, add on another week for premenstrual tension, emotional upheavals, insecurities and paranoia; that on top of this we also get on with our relationships, work, look after the house, kids, friends and stroke everyone else's ego whilst this is going on. Frankly, I came to the realisation that us woman are F@@@ing Incredible!

You may well laugh that it's taken me so long to truly realise this, but yes I can honestly say that morning was like an Epiphany! The height of emotion that came together for that one insight was immense.

WHY? Because what my menstrual cycle had brought together in that rage filled time was years and years of pent up emotions, of listening to, resisting to, but ultimately accepting all the demands made on me not just in that week or that month but throughout my life. All of which I accepted as normal and OK, because that's what I'd been conditioned to believe from being a little girl.

And yet this morning an invisible line had been crossed and like most events that change your life, immense clarity came from reaching the other side of that line.

I realised I wasn't just a pre-menopausal woman going through the change. I was suddenly able to see, hear, smell, and touch the contamination of what I had been subjecting myself to for over 40+ years and it was vile! It was so vile it made me feel physically ill and livid that I had spent so much of my life buying into something which was just total (for me) Bollocks. (Yes that's how livid I was.... I kept swearing to myself).

My 80 year old mother had just gone back home from spending 5 weeks living with us, which with 3 teenage boys, a partner and 2 dogs and visitors in the middle, and my mum poorly during this time, was quite a squeeze and altered the family dynamics considerably. However, we managed really well and to be fair I thought she would have been with us for much longer this time.

This was probably the 4th time in 12 months she had been with us and each time was more difficult than the last. Why? Because she would only leave her beloved home when she couldn't cope with living with my father any more. At 80 and he at 84 this was some feat.

Alcohol was a chronic problem and we all had our own way of dealing with it, and being conditioned to "put up and shut up" with this situation, was one of them.

This was a no win situation and all we could do was keep my mum as positive as possible, support her and remove her from the situation as often as possible over the years. This in itself was exhausting and it took its toll on my relationships at home, work, romantically and friends.

I had been taught to obey my father and mother and not voice an opinion out loud because children were to be seen and not heard. But, I had stopped listening, and had been disagreeing for years with the conversations, arguments and how they lived their lives and what they portrayed to the outside world.

So what made me so LIVID?

The sudden realisation that my old belief system was still ruling my life and I thought I was so independent and resilient after everything I'd been through. I knew it had impacted on every single relationship I had ever had, as I my mood changed as soon as I'd been to visit my parents. My barriers went right back up again and straight into defence mode which I had started to realise was impacting on my current relationship as I constantly went back into self-sabotage mode. I was now though actually ready to get to the core of it! It's only take over 40 years but I was finally ready to deal with it."

We cannot underestimate the lessons we are given in life and how we tackle them. If we still have our filters on, then it's impossible to see what's right in front of us. Just shifting that perspective and Bridging the Gap using Energy Therapy makes an impact for life and there is no going back, or if there is, it's now done consciously as those filters have gone now. There's no more excuses.

However, we have to be ready to face the filters coming off as facing those truths feels unsafe and we are programmed to keep safe at all times. Energy Therapy enables you that safety. Energy Therapy brings forth all that courage that's already there inside you. It just needs a little help to pop out and look after you in the right way.

For me this filter, as for most people, came out in anger. If I had not already done a considerable amount of Energy Work on clearing out old issues prior to this, Anger may have completely fuelled a very different reaction from me. Not being able to sit with it and assess where it had come from but react in an unhealthy way. Taking it out on others, storming off in the car, going into fight, flight or freeze mode.

How do you react to anger or have done in the past? How do people you know react? Sometimes, it can be unpleasant to look back and see our reactions in the light of day.

Try to list some of the events that are still really clear to you in your mind as if you can still feel them, see them and hear them. Then go through truthfully on what your reaction actually was at the time (not what you'd have liked it to have been).

EVENT	REACTION (Notes)

These are issues for you to start working on in the charts or with a practitioner. Once cleared or faced, notice any changes and let us know how you've got on.

"This experience for me which was so vivid was that my belief system was that my father should be respected, believed, honoured and obeyed at all times, as should my mother. I love my parents deeply and for 40+ years I had tried valiantly, painfully to please them and do what they expected of me and most of the time without being conscious of what I was doing.

I was confused completely for most of this time on the language they used and then the actions they took, which just didn't tally up and refused to make sense to me.

How can love result in such toxic behaviour? This on top of my own topsy turvey life, left me stumbling, falling over and ending up on my knees. It's when you're there looking up, you realise who's truly there for you and no matter what my mum was there! Through thick and thin, at the end of the phone, in person, with cake, tea, or that precious hug. She's always been there.

Working as an Energy Therapist led me to work with all sorts of clients as well as working on myself and as you help others clear out their past blockages it cannot but help you release your own along the way. Even if you think you've dealt with them it's amazing what comes up.

I had cleared so much over the years and yet I knew I had not yet faced my dad and my blockages there. I was avoiding it. Not that it was scary anymore but that I was just so exhausted from it all. 40 years of arguments and wasted energy I really didn't want to go there anymore and give it more time.

Yet that morning, of my cycle, I was so livid! I'd been able to separate each and every situation and realise that it had nothing to do with my menstrual cycle, my partner, or my kids and it was all about my dad. It had finally reached a point where I needed to clear these blockages so I could move on freely from the past.

I realised I had heard the same things over and over again from him. His opinions, his version of the truth, his anger, his version of love, his projection of guilt onto us, how we all talked crap and didn't have a clue what we were talking about. This toxic, very toxic, behaviour, made him do and say anything for his whiskey and his own way. We tried everything over the years to help him get dry and for a few weeks it would work, then he'd get bored and go back to his old ways and because I loved him so much and knew the beautiful soul he was underneath all this toxic behaviour, and my mum, I accepted that's just the way it is. And we'd try again some time later, year after year, after year.

Things were changing however, slowly, and mum was listening to us more and more and spending more time with me away from him. Hence the 5 Weeks with me, but by the 4th week, he was back in hospital in a dreadful state. He amazes us every time he goes in to A&E that he manages to come back out again. There is a strong will to survive in this man. It gives me an understanding of how mind over matter actually works physically.

I had not visited him for some time, neither had my mum. I fact she has not seen him since and probably never will now. I managed 10 minutes in the hospital before I had to walk out not able to listen to his toxicity as he started again. I managed another 10 minutes when I visited him in the Residential Home before he resorted to shouting, sneering and talking about money and whiskey again. This gap of not seeing him then going back into that totally toxic environment really gave me clarity.

My filters were finally off.... I could see. It was like going back into hell and I finally realised I didn't belong there in any way, shape or form.

I went home and Tapped on myself for 40 minutes on how I felt about the situation. I cried, I yawned, I sobbed, I coughed, I choked and lost my voice. I felt drained, empty and wanted to sleep but I continued to worked through it.

I came out with Loving... Toxic... Family..... Family? What the ffff is that... family...what a joke!"

Each word we use means something different to each of us.

Family what does it really mean to you? What would you like it to mean? Is it loving? Is it toxic? Is it both like mine?

Perhaps that's our journey...... our real purpose in life. To actually work out over our life time how to bridge the gap to make it loving and stay loving from our perspective and our perspective alone. We cannot force someone elses.

We all have a little bit of toxic in our life and it does cause stress but not all stress is bad stress. It depends on what you do with it.

"I will be going to see my father, it's his birthday soon and I will be able to bridge the gap with love now that I have worked it through. I will be able to thank him for his painful life journey that I have had to be part of so that I could grow into the being I am today. It would not have brought my brother and I together as close as we are now. I would not have met the people I've been so blessed to have had in my life or have had or the experiences I've had or be able to deal with them in the way I do now, if I hadn't had to watch and be part of his painful journey. If he had to live this life with such pain and loneliness for his daughter and sons' life lesson to be to bridge the gap and do things differently then I believe that's been achieved."

What life lessons are your family members teaching you?

TREASURE HUNT

Our Treasure Hunt of Life is to find the gems we've left behind each door of experience along the way. To accept our journey and then to take back and polish up each recovered emotional gem so it gleams with pride turning self-doubt into Freedom then Joy.

The outside environment you put yourself in, or are put in as a child, has a massive effect on your life. Freeing yourself of those chains, of other people's beliefs, that over time become our own, is not easy but it truly is the most liberating feeling in the world when you become YOU, truly YOU, your authentic YOU for the first time in your life.

There is no restriction on time limit for this happening either. Some may be blessed to achieve this as a child (my aim to help this happen), some as a young adult and then there's us, the over 40's and MY don't we appreciate that liberation all the more when we get there.

So remember: Life spirals flow at different speeds too. Sometimes we seem stuck in the same lesson for a very long time (**note**: maybe time to Awaken again) and others speed by before we get a real chance to relish them.

With this in mind, understand that in time, our paths (especially with those left behind) may cross again, with more beauty and understanding and harmony than ever before. Once you're on this journey it's pureness, beauty and simplicity are what inspires us to sustain it....

Awaken, Engage, Transform, Inspire and Sustain...... it's the spiral of life.

ROUND UP

To finalise what has been given so far let's do a quick breakdown of what my outcomes have been from this to help you assess your own later on.

1) The realisation **(AWAKE)** that until I started using and working with Energy Therapies I did not have the ability to communicate effectively with anyone in my life to sustain a loving and lasting relationship as I wished to.

2) **(Engage)** My outside environment was impacting on me from childhood and I did not have the tools to shield myself from them so it kept repeating until I learnt how to deal with it, from each stage listed.

3) **(Engage)** This resulted in my triggers building year after year for decades as my logic tried to overcome my senses.

4) **(Engage)** This resulted in decades of feeling so unworthy I didn't believe I was able to achieve any end goal. This pervaded my whole being but evaded my conscious thought because it was so deeply hidden.

5) **(Transform)** I learnt how to melt my fight, flight and freeze ice bergs by retuning my strings.

> Ie: releasing, guilt, shame, resentment, jealousy, abandonment, failure, not being good enough or worthy enough to deserve more. This treasure hunt I went on in took me on a sensory journey through my body & mind that I have learnt to trust and love about myself.

6) **(Transform & Inspire)** Releasing all this guilt, shame, resentment, jealousy and other negative emotions allowed me to raise my vibrational frequency to move forward and finally achieve an end result. (This handbook)!

7) **(Sustain)** I am still learning to clear out new emotions and experiences as they come along.

8) **(Awake)** This Spiral to raise me up further is one I am more conscious of and one I understand I cannot and do not wish to do alone.

9) **(Awake, Engage, Transform, Sustain)** I now recognise I need help too, and once a season (at least), make sure I work with an Energy Therapist to have a good clear out myself on top of the work I do on my own.

I have learnt this is an exhilarating and freeing journey from a past I didn't even realise was holding me back, It was just my life.

NOW I can achieve more than I ever imagined possible if I put my focus to it and keep going through adversity with skills to help me bounce back quicker and with more compassion each time.

REMINDER

As you start to undertake this journey, PLEASE do not underestimate the power of your energy system and how some of the symptoms listed in the Awareness Charts may make you feel. There is huge intensity in who we all are and what we feel. It can be very overwhelming to deal with if we do not understand where it has come from.

This is especially the case for children and teenagers who are experiencing the intensity of emotions for the first time. When they react with BIG behavioural issues, remind yourself of the points attached and perhaps ask them if this is the first time they have felt like this?

If it is when they are calm enough giving them an explanation to what is happening in their energy system. It is something they will certainly understand, especially the physical symptoms.

If it is not the first time they have experienced these symptoms, then work should be done in a very gentle way to clear past issues and the present ones. Colours and shapes work very well here.

Again, I always recommend children and teenagers work with a professional Energy therapist to help them feel safe throughout the process.

NOTE:

This book and charts are a step back from the Gary Craig EFT (Emotional Freedom Technique) way to work and incorporates some of the regular EFT towards the end of the handbook.

This has been created to give families the ability to connect together when one person is struggling and understand what and why they may be going through as they use the charts.

This brings families together in a more compassionate and understanding way to face the changes ahead together.

You are not alone.

What you feel is not something only you feel. We are all connected and as human beings we all experience each of the emotions listed in the charts and much more throughout our lives. We will just experience them at different times scales and different events, throughout our life. It is important that we give each other the compassion to grow and learn from each stage.

This step back from Gary Craig's EFT method is to allow individuals and families to understand that all the emotions listed are actually, normal experiences (although some unpleasant) to go through in life.

It is learning to deal with them in an effective way which allows you to move forward in life in a kinder, compassionate, loving and truthful way with yourself and then others.

Shall we begin ......

DISCLAIMER: These charts are a starting point to break down barriers for Therapists and individuals. Deep issues should always be worked through with a certified Energy therapist, EFT practitioner in a safe environment.

These are not a Medical Documents and have not been authorised by any Medical Body. It is purely Energy Therapy information researched and sourced through EFT, Reiki, Chinese Medicine and Energy Medicine sources.

If you have a medical condition it is recommended you check in with your doctor before, during and after you start using these methods.

METHODS OF USE - TAP AROUND THE CLOCK

1. SIDE EFFECTS

Are there any side effects to Tapping?

Do not underestimate the power of your energy system. You are more powerful than you could ever imagine and you are just starting on that journey of discovery.

You nor I, know what you will clear and with what force until you start the process. Every single one of us are different and that is what makes us unique. Yes, we may all have similar emotions and physical problems but how our system deals with them and clearing them will be unique to your life experiences.

Remember your system may have been asleep for a very long time. If this is the case, much the same as any detox programme, releases may come out of every available space they can. Here are some examples:-
- Hot or cold or tingly fingers, feet, eyes, ears and skin
- Yawning
- Burping and breaking wind
- Tightness, discomfort, pain (uncomfortable but when tapped through it's an amazing release) in chest, throat, stomach, back shoulders etc
- Laughing,
- Watery eyes (crying)
- Bloating
- Nausea
- Shaking
- Clearing out of the bladder and bowels
- An argument

These symptoms may come on immediately or over the first week you start Tapping and are perfectly normal as your energy system starts to adjust to its new regime.

Be gently with yourself and give yourself time to adjust. Say thank you for each new release as you tap it out of your system. Understand that this was inside you, trapped and fighting for freedom and now it's escaping, running away. Let it go..... freely.... Gratefully.

If possible, do not restrain it and try to squash it back in.

If this thought frightens you work with a Practitioner so they can keep you safe.

2. FEELING SAFE

It is important to always monitor and feel safe whilst doing any Energy work and it's the same for Tapping.

If you are feeling vulnerable, then it is advised to Tap with someone. Find someone your trust to Tap with you or do this with an EFT Practitioner.

Evaluate your levels of intensity of the feelings you are having from 10 being the highest and 0 being the lowest. If it is nearer 10 then perhaps work with someone.

Use this system of evaluation throughout each round of the Tapping process to monitor your progress. Write it down to access at the end of the session.

3. SAFETY METHOD

If you are feeling a very high intensity of emotion/pain and do not have someone to tap with immediately, then this system may be used until you are with someone who can assist you.

1) Tap on your Karate Chop point (Soft Side of hand – See EFT chart for points) and say:

"Even though I have all these feelings all over my body I accept that they are there and I accept me"

"Even though I have all these feelings all over my body I am now putting them in a secure place (eg: Box / Cave / Rocket /The moon) and I am securing them in with (10 inch nails / Massive boulders / Plasma) and making it secure until I am ready to deal with all these feelings." Repeat x 2

2) Tap on a Short Circuit of the flowing points repeating these short phrases"

Top of eyebrow:	All these Feelings
Side of Eye:	All over my body
Under eye:	All these Feelings
Under Nose:	Make Them Secure
On Chin:	Make Them Secure
Under Collar Bone:	In this Box/cave/Rocket
Under Arm:	In this Box / Cave / Rocket
Top of The Head:	All these feelings Seal them in

Repeat this until you feel calmer and safer and able to work with someone or able to work alone a little further.

This method of Tapping is the usual version of EFT and can be used at any point to Tap with for emotions and physical pain just take away the rocket/cave/box.

Www.live4energy.co.uk

NEGATIVE HEALTH AWARENESS

Family Tap & Thrive

Karate Chop set up point

Top of Head Governing Point

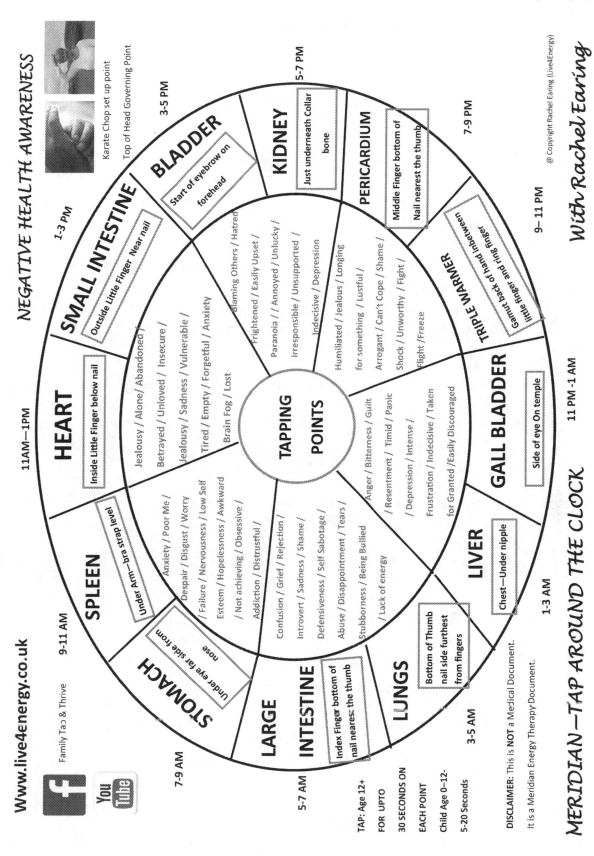

TAPPING POINTS

BLADDER 3-5 PM
Start of eyebrow on forehead

KIDNEY 5-7 PM
Just underneath Collar bone

PERICARDIUM 7-9 PM
Middle Finger bottom of Nail nearest the thumb

SMALL INTESTINE 1-3 PM
Outside Little Finger Near nail

HEART 11AM—1PM
Inside Little Finger below nail

SPLEEN 9-11 AM
Under Arm—bra strap level

STOMACH 7-9 AM
Under eye far side from nose

LARGE INTESTINE 5-7 AM
Index Finger bottom of nail nearest the thumb

LUNGS 3-5 AM
Bottom of Thumb nail side furthest from fingers

LIVER 1-3 AM
Chest—Under nipple

GALL BLADDER 11 PM -1 AM
Side of eye On temple

TRIPLE WARMER 9— 11 PM
Gamut back of hand inbetween little finger and ring finger

Blaming Others / Hatred / Frightened / Easily Upset / Paranoia / / Annoyed / Unlucky / Irresponsible / Unsupported / Indecisive / Depression

Humiliated / Jealous / Longing for something / Lustful / Arrogant / Can't Cope / Shame / Shock / Unworthy / Fight / Flight /Freeze

Anger / Bitterness / Guilt / Resentment / Timid / Panic / Depression / Intense / Frustration / Indecisive / Taken for Granted /Easily Discouraged

Jealousy / Alone/ Abandoned / Betrayed / Unloved / Insecure / Jealousy / Sadness / Vulnerable / Tired / Empty / Forgetful / Anxiety / Brain Fog / Lost

Anxiety / Poor Me / Despair / Disgust / Worry / Failure / Nervousness / Low Self Esteem / Hopelessness / Awkward / Not achieving / Obsessive / Addiction / Distrustful /

Confusion / Grief / Rejection / Introvert / Sadness / Shame / Defensiveness / Self Sabotage / Abuse / Disappointment / Tears / Stubborness / Being Bullied / Lack of energy

TAP: Age 12+
FOR UPTO
30 SECONDS ON
EACH POINT
Child Age 0–12-
5-20 Seconds

DISCLAIMER: This is **NOT** a Medical Document.
It is a Meridian Energy Therapy Document.

MERIDIAN—TAP AROUND THE CLOCK

With Rachel Earing

@ Copyright Rachel Earing (Live4Energy)

4. ENERGY CLEANSER & JET LAG METHOD (USED ON APP)

(Cleanse your system or for Jet Lag Tap repeat 3 times a day until adjusted).

This is perfect when your short on time and wanting a quick clear out or need to re- adjust your system to the timescale you are in.

Tap for up to 30 seconds on each point clockwise (less for children – see Tapping With Children)
1) Time to synchronise yourself with where you are. Check the time on your watch.
2) Look at the chart and see what it corresponds to ie: between 0700-0900am it is Stomach Meridian time.
3) Start Tapping on that timescale area ie: Stomach Meridian (Tap under eye) and tap for approximately 30 seconds or more
4) Once you have completed this Meridian move onto the next Meridian in a clockwise direction until you have Tapped on all Points from where you started.

For Jet Lag repeat 2 or 3 times a day until you are adjusted.

Used daily and as many times as you wish this will help blockages in your system clear naturally and your energy system will start to flow more freely as it develops and recognises that you are talking to it in a language it understands.

This system helps to raise to the surface issues/events/people which may need more detailed work on. As this happens be aware this is a natural process.

Move onto others Methods to clear further as issues appear.

THIS MAY ALSO BE USED FOR NIGHT SHIFT ADJUSTMENT.
1) To keep alert reverse the Tapping points for the time of day you are in.
2) So if you start the Night Shift at 7pm. Start Tapping at 7am and tap around the clock until 1 circuit has been completed.
3) Repeat as necessary.
4) The same applies to adjust back to day times once you have had some sleep.

5. DAILY CLEANSE CROSS OVER METHOD (EFT METHOD)

This technique is literally as it says Tap from your Head point all the way down to your hands. This includes the usual tapping pattern for an EFT workout, plus a couple of extra points for a fuller clearance.

You do not need to follow the clock for this to work. Tapping and crossing over of energy meridians helps keep your system healthy and out of parallel mode which can be a depressed state of body and mind.

Tap all these points for upto 30 seconds with intention to clear and revitalise:

1) Tap the Top of your Head
2) Top of Eyebrows
3) Side of eye Temple
4) Under eye
5) Under nose
6) On Chin
7) Under Collar bone
8) Under Arm
9) Under Nail Thumb opposite fingers
10) Under Nail on Index Finger nearest the thumb
11) Under Middle Finger Nearest the thumb
12) Under Ring Finger Nail (next to little finger)
13) Under Nail on Outside of Little Finger
14) Gamut Point (back of hand soft spot in between little and ring finger)
15) Middle of chest bone (Extra point – This is your Thymus Gland responsible for hormones and thyroid gland)

This is great first thing in the morning or between 3-5pm in the afternoon when we have that lull time in our energy levels (ie siesta time) or whenever that lull hits you and you've still got so much more to fit in to the day.

6. HOLD AND BREATHE METHOD

Holding your points helps to calm down and sedate your system. This is perfect for Insomniacs, anxiety attacks and those suffering from chronic pain.

Holding each point for up to 20-30 seconds is ample time. Children and Infants will not need this length of time so adjust appropriately in between 2 and 20 seconds.

You may use all these points or just pick a couple that you can reach if you are in bed

sleepy and don't want to think about it too much.

1) HOLD the Top of your Head
2) HOLD Top of Eyebrows
3) HOLD Side of eye Temple
4) HOLD Under eye
5) HOLD Under nose
6) HOLD On Chin
7) HOLD Under Collar bone
8) HOLD Under Arm
9) HOLD Under Nail Thumb opposite fingers
10) HOLD Under Nail on Index Finger nearest the thumb
11) HOLD Under Middle Finger Nearest the thumb
12) HOLD Under Ring Finger Nail (next to little finger)
13) HOLD Under Nail on Outside of Little Finger
14) HOLD Gamut Point (back of hand in between little and ring finger)
15) HOLD Middle of chest bone (Extra point – This is your Thymus Gland responsible for hormones and thyroid gland)

This can be done on just 1 or 2 points, some or all of them. You will feel the effects and know when you've done enough.

7. EMOTIONAL AWARENESS TAPPING

This technique is great for working with alone or within a group. For those who know EFT already it follows the pattern of Tearless Trauma / Borrowing Benefits but without selecting an individual to work with.

It allows you to start the tapping process without having to tune into yourself too much and let's your subconscious do the work for you.

1) Start tapping on your Karate Chop point and prepare your system to start engaging.
2) Check the time and look at the emotions in the corresponding Meridian point: ie 0900-1100am SPLEEN time
3) As you are Tapping look at the Emotions & Physical Charts. Pick out 1 or 2 of the emotions/physical ailments which resonate with you at this time and let yourself engage with a particular incident, person, place that these emotions connect to. Don't worry if you can't just Tap on the emotions/ailment anyway your subconscious will make a connection for you. Feel free to adjust the wording on the emotions to suit you and your family.
4) Now start Tapping on the corresponding Meridian point (Spleen under arm) Say out loud the following phrases:

   "Even though I have felt Anxious, worried or disgusted at "that" (let "that" represent the event or person you're thinking of) I accept that's how it is and I accept me. X 2

   Even though I have felt anxious, worried, or disgusted at "that" I wonder if it's safe for me to let go now. That's ok and I'm ok whatever I decide. because it's my choice". "I will know"

5) Tap until it feels comfortable to move onto the next Meridian moving in a clockwise direction and start again on the next Meridian. Be aware that emotions share some of the same Meridians see point 6.
6) If covering the same emotions over 2 Meridian Points you may Tap alternately between these 2 points repeating the phrases as point 4. Ie; Heart and Small Intestine share emotions so tap alternately on Inside Little finger and Outside Little Finger.
7) Carry on Tapping around in a Clockwise direction until you have completed the whole clock. If possible, Finish you tapping with an affirmation of your choice.

Used daily and as many times as you wish this will help blockages in your system clear naturally and your energy system will start to flow more freely as it develops and recognises that you are talking to it in a language it understands.

This system helps to raise to the surface issues/events/people which may need more detailed work on. As this happens be aware this is a natural process and clear as appropriate.

Take a measure of how you are feeling in intensity before you begin with 10 being the highest and 0 being the lowest and repeat again if you wish.

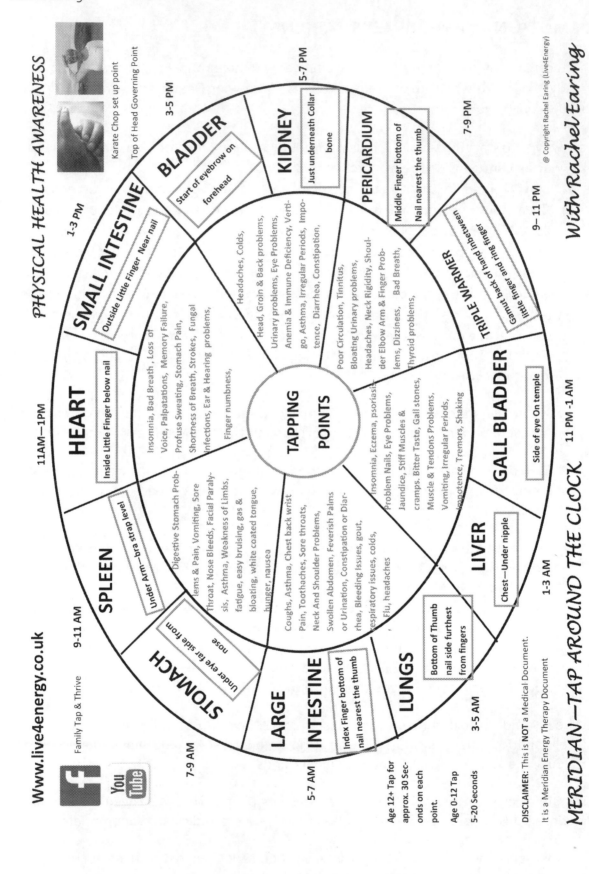

PHYSICAL HEALTH AWARENESS

With Rachel Earing

MERIDIAN—TAP AROUND THE CLOCK

Www.live4energy.co.uk

Karate Chop set up point
Top of Head Governing Point

BLADDER 3-5 PM
Start of eyebrow on forehead

SMALL INTESTINE 1-3 PM
Outside Little Finger Near nail

KIDNEY 5-7 PM
Just underneath Collar bone

PERICARDIUM 7-9 PM
Middle Finger bottom of Nail nearest the thumb

HEART 11AM—1PM
Inside Little Finger below nail

TRIPLE WARMER 9—11 PM
Gamut back of hand inbetween little finger and ring finger

SPLEEN 9-11 AM
Under Arm—bra strap level

GALL BLADDER 11 PM -1 AM
Side of eye On temple

STOMACH 7-9 AM
Under eye far side from nose

LIVER 1-3 AM
Chest—Under nipple

LARGE INTESTINE 5-7 AM
Index Finger bottom of nail nearest the thumb

LUNGS 3-5 AM
Bottom of Thumb nail side furthest from fingers

TAPPING POINTS

Headaches, Colds,

Head, Groin & Back problems, Urinary problems, Eye Problems, Anemia & Immune Deficiency, Vertigo, Asthma, Irregular Periods, Impotence, Diarrhea, Constipation,

Insomnia, Bad Breath , Loss of Voice, Palpatations, Memory Failure, Profuse Sweating, Stomach Pain, Shortness of Breath, Strokes, Fungal Infections, Ear & Hearing problems, Finger numbness,

Poor Circulation, Tinnitus, Bloating Urinary problems, Headaches, Neck Rigidity, Shoulder Elbow Arm & Finger Problems, Dizziness, Bad Breath, Thyroid problems,

Digestive Stomach Problems & Pain, Vomiting, Sore Throat, Nose Bleeds, Facial Paralysis, Asthma, Weakness of Limbs, fatigue, easy bruising, gas & bloating, white coated tongue, hunger, nausea

Insomnia, Eczema, psoriasis, Problem Nails, Eye Problems, Jaundice, Bitter Taste, Gall stones, cramps, Stiff Muscles & Muscle & Tendons Problems, Vomiting, Irregular Periods, Impotence, Tremors, Shaking

Coughs, Asthma, Chest back wrist Pain, Toothaches, Sore throats, Neck And Shoulder Problems, Swollen Abdomen, Feverish Palms or Urination, Constipation or Diarrhea, Bleeding Issues, gout, respiratory issues, colds, Flu, headaches

Family Tap & Thrive

Age 12+ Tap for approx. 30 Seconds on each point.

Age 0-12 Tap 5-20 Seconds

8. PHYSICAL AWARENESS TAPPING METHOD

If you have physical pain or discomfort in your body, be specific in identifying where it is and what it feels like eg: butterflies in my tummy, knot in my right shoulder.

1) Find the appropriate meridian eg Stomach Meridian and start Tapping on this meridian.
2) Use the phrase "Even though I have these eg: "butterflies in my tummy" I accept that I do because I do and I accept me" X 2 or 3 times
3) Short Sequence Tapping

Top of eyebrow:	All these "butterflies"
Side of Eye:	All over my tummy
Under eye:	All these butterflies
Under Nose:	All over my tummy
On Chin:	I accept them
Under Collar Bone:	All these butterflies
Under Arm:	All over my tummy
Top of The Head:	These Butterflies all over my tummy

4) Each Meridian passes through a physical part of the body so just choose the nearest Meridian to the part of the body which is uncomfortable or in pain and then then do a short sequence until the pain moves somewhere else or down in intensity.
5) Repeat the process identifying where the physical discomfort has moved to or repeat in same place if required. Finish with an affirmation (positive).

Take a measure of how you are feeling in intensity with 10 being the highest and 0 being the lowest and repeat again to get as low as possible.

This system helps to raise to the surface issues/events/people which may need more detailed work on. As this happens be aware this is a natural process and clear as appropriate.

9. TAPPING WITH CHILDREN

Added Benefit Learning to Tell The Time.
- Tap Around The Clock is perfect for engaging young children into learning to tell the time and engage with what is happening in their body at the same time.
- Would your life have had added benefits if you'd had this tool as you were growing up?

(All of the other methods can be used with children just reduce the tapping time (Infants 2-5 taps on each points and ages 5-12 perhaps 3-9 Taps on each point, let them decide) age 12 upwards (their choice) 5 taps to 30 seconds and finish with an affirmation if possible.)
- Children don't always want to Tap or be Tapped on especially when they're upset. If this is the case just tap on yourself, near them or use a picture, favourite toy or just use one tapping point (eg karate chop) and engage them when they're ready.
- Holding the points may be an alternative they choose instead.
- Tapping only on positive emotions is perfect for children and works just as effectively. (see Positive chart).

Using the POSITIVE CHART you do NOT need to use "even though".

Just go straight into "I am Kind. I am funny. I am strong" etc...

Start
1) Check the time on your watch and start Tapping on the corresponding Meridian to the time.
2) Tap on each point, or on a toy, posters or yourself if the child does not want to be tapped on. Less time is required the younger the child up-to 2-5 taps on each point is fine on an infant.
   Tap slowly to bring down any anxiety the slower you tap the more it helps to bring down the energy flow.
   The faster you tap the more it raises the energy level point.
3) "Even though I have all these horrid feelings inside and I accept they're there, I know I am also strong and powerful and Kind and funny and that is what I choose to be" Repeat x 3
4) Let the child pick out the emotions from each meridian then ask them to use the Tapping point of that meridian in the Positive chart as you Tap Around The Clock or use the toy, poster etc.
5) If the child/teen resists the positives and doesn't feel they are true, then go back to the Negative/Physical Charts and let them select symptoms from there.
6) Then tap on the:

"Even though I have a sore throat and cough/confused and sad (Large Intestine/ Lungs Meridian chose as appropriate for the time scale etc). I accept that I do because I do and I accept me anyway.

Repeat this 3 times then move onto the next meridian until they have tapped around the clock.

(optional) It may be too much to do the short circuit too but if they are willing them add this in after each meridian.

Top of eyebrow:	This sore throat and cough
Side of Eye:	Confused and sad
Under eye:	This sore throat and cough
Under Nose:	This sore throat and cough
On Chin:	Confused and sad
Under Collar Bone:	This sore throat and cough
Under Arm:	This sore throat and cough
Top of The Head:	Confused and Sad

For serious emotional issues with a child it is always advised to work with a Practitioner.

Take a measure of how you are feeling in intensity with 10 being the highest and 0 being the lowest and repeat again to get as low as possible.

This system helps to raise to the surface issues/events/people which may need more detailed work on. As this happens be aware this is a natural process and clear as appropriate.

POSITIVE EMOTIONAL AWARENESS

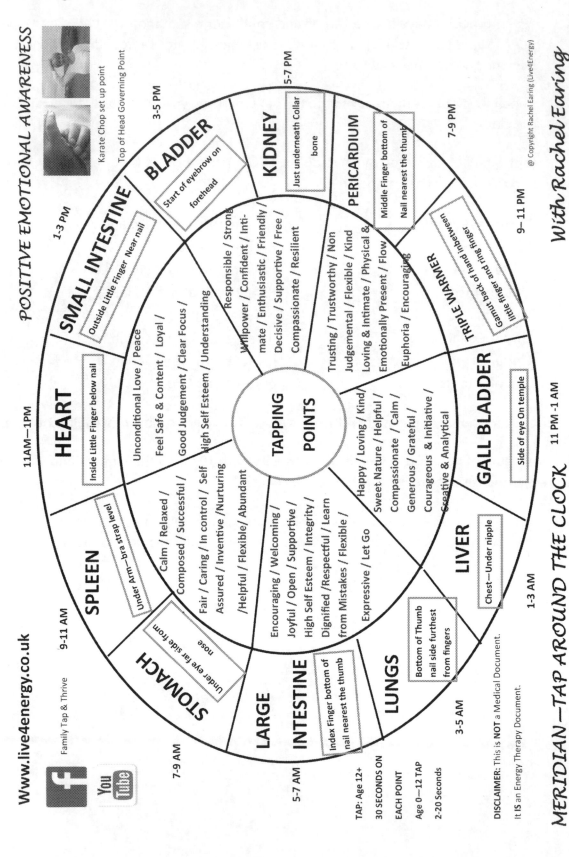

Karate Chop set up point

Top of Head Governing Point

Www.live4energy.co.uk

Family Tap & Thrive

BLADDER 3-5 PM
Start of eyebrow on forehead

SMALL INTESTINE 1-3 PM
Outside Little Finger Near nail

KIDNEY 5-7 PM
Just underneath Collar bone

PERICARDIUM 7-9 PM
Middle Finger bottom of Nail nearest the thumb

TRIPLE WARMER 9—11 PM
Gamut back of hand inbetween little finger and ring finger

HEART 11AM—1PM
Inside Little Finger below nail

Willpower / Confident / Inti-mate / Enthusiastic / Friendly / Decisive / Supportive / Free / Compassionate / Resilient

Responsible / Strong

Unconditional Love / Peace

Feel Safe & Content / Loyal / Good Judgement / Clear Focus / High Self Esteem / Understanding

Trusting / Trustworthy / Non Judgemental / Flexible / Kind Loving & Intimate / Physical & Emotionally Present / Flow Euphoria / Encouraging

TAPPING POINTS

SPLEEN 9-11 AM
Under Arm—bra strap level

Calm / Relaxed / Composed / Successful / Fair / Caring / In control / Self Assured / Inventive /Nurturing /Helpful / Flexible/ Abundant

Happy / Loving / Kind/ Sweet Nature / Helpful / Compassionate / Calm / Generous / Grateful / Courageous & Initiative / Creative & Analytical

GALL BLADDER 11 PM -1 AM
Side of eye On temple

STOMACH 7-9 AM
Under eye far side from nose

Encouraging / Welcoming / Joyful / Open / Supportive / High Self Esteem / Integrity / Dignified /Respectful / Learn from Mistakes / Flexible / Expressive / Let Go

LIVER 1-3 AM
Chest—Under nipple

LARGE INTESTINE 5-7 AM
Index Finger bottom of nail nearest the thumb

LUNGS 3-5 AM
Bottom of Thumb nail side furthest from fingers

TAP: Age 12+
30 SECONDS ON EACH POINT
Age 0—12 TAP
2-20 Seconds

DISCLAIMER: This is **NOT** a Medical Document.
It **IS** an Energy Therapy Document.

@ Copyright Rachel Earing (Live4Energy)

With Rachel Earing

MERIDIAN—TAP AROUND THE CLOCK

10. ALTERNATE TAPPING (YING/YANG) / & BEDTIME

- This is perfect for short burst Tapping rather than the full sequence if your short on time and it still balances out your Ying and Yang (Alternate Meridians).
- It is perfect for children when you wish to cover the "through the night points" where they're waking up, not going to bed, over tired etc.
- This method covers the time scale you are in and the opposing time scale so you are covering your weak and strong meridians.

This is especially good for your Triple Warmer and Spleen Meridian as they are usually in quite a lot of conflict.

YING/YANG TAPPING

1) Start at time scale you are in (eg Triple Warmer - gamut point) and pick out a few emotions/physical ailments and start to tap on clearing them or emphasising them if they are positive ones.

2) Use these type of phrases or pick your own:
   "Even though I have these emotions/physical pain I accept they are there and (if negative) I accept me just as I am. OR If positive – Drop the even though and just go into "I am kind, loving and Flexible". Repeat x 2

3) Then move to the SPLEEN meridian (opposing point) and pick out 2 or 3 emotions/physical pain repeat the same process

   ie: "I am calm, relaxed and composed" I release despair, disgust, worry / bloating, nausea, hunger etc). Finish with an affirmation (positive).

By tapping on the alternate points you are still strengthening your system but just concentrating on 2 or 4 points each time.

11. ABSTRACT TAPPING

This is perfect for anyone who has an affinity with colours/shapes or numbers rather than emotions and leads onto the traditional EFT method of Tapping more fluidly so please feel free to go straight into this method if you are familiar with it.

1) Take note of the time of day/night you are in before you start to Tap.

2) Use the Tap Around The Clock to start Tapping from ie: 3am-5am Lung Meridian (thumb point) and make a note of how your intensity values are (10 highest and 0 lowest,). Tune into your body and if in a high state of intensity note what you see or hear or if you don't see anything the first colour, shape, number, sound, which comes to mind. And if possible where it relates to in your body.

3) Use these type of phrases: "Even though I have this colour, shape, number in my "right shoulder I accept that's how it is and I accept me"

"Even though I have this colour, shape, number at the moment I accept they are here and I accept me anyway."

Repeat x 3

4) Short Sequence plus Top of Head:

Top of eyebrow:	All these "colours, shapes"
Side of Eye:	All these "numbers"
Under eye:	All in my "?"
Under Nose:	Numbers, shapes, ect
On Chin:	right shoulder etc"
Under Collar Bone:	All these "Colours, shapes"
Under Arm:	All these "numbers"
Top of The Head:	"Right shoulder etc"

5) Tune into your body after each sequence and see where the abstract image has moved to and what it is now (it may well change and move), or is it the same?

6) Tap again using the script above but with the new information ie: Green circle in left knee and Repeat points 3) and 4) as required.

7) Repeat until the abstract has disappeared or gone down in intensity to as low as possible.

Take a measure of how you are feeling in intensity with 10 being the highest and 0 being the lowest and repeat again to get as low as possible.

This system helps to raise to the surface issues/events/people which may need more detailed work on. As this happens be aware this is a natural process and clear as appropriate.

12. MAKING CONNECTIONS (THE APP ENABLES THIS PROCESS TOO)

Using all the charts together, you will start to make connections and this is the exciting part.

Start Tapping

- Pick out 1 or 2 emotions from a specific Meridian point.
  EG: Heart Meridian – Emotions – Lost and Abandoned
- Or Pick out 2 physical ailments from the same Meridian which may relate to these emotions:
  EG: Heart Meridian – Physical – Palpatations, Insomnia
- Or Pick out 2 positive emotions from the Positive chart same Meridan. EG: Heart Meridian – Positive – Feeling Safe, Unconditional Love
- Start Tapping on the point and use this Phrase:

  "Even though I have felt "Lost and Abandoned and I've had Palpatations and insomnia (*use words you prefer for each symptom listed such as "can't sleep" rather than insomnia, if you wish*) when "That" happened". I Accept that it did because it did and I love and accept me anyway".

  If using the Positive Chart: State the following type script:

  "I am safe. I am loved, I give unconditional love, I am safe".

  Repeat 3 times
- Short Sequence: (always include the Meridian point you are working on here)

Short Sequence:

Top of Eyebrow	Lost and Abandoned / I am Safe & loved
Side of Eye:	Palpations and insomnia / I give Unconditional love
Under Eye:	Lost and Abandoned / I am Safe and Loved
Under Nose:	Palpations and Insomnia / I give Unconditional Love
On Chin:	repeat
Underneath Collar Bone:	Lost, abandoned, Palpations, Insomnia, Safe, Loved
Under Arm	Repeat
Inside Little Finger	Lost and Abandoned / Safe, Loved, unconditional
Outside Little Finger	Palpations and Insomnia / Safe, Loved Unconditionally

Repeat if required or move onto the next meridian.

13. TAPPING SPEEDS

- When you Tap slower it may calm you down
- When you Tap faster it may energise you.

  So depending on what you wish to achieve be aware of how quickly you are tapping.
- With Anxiety and stress, you will probably start tapping quite quickly. Slow it down to help yourself stay calmer through the process and the same for children.
- If you are lethargic and tired throughout the day. You may wish to tap more quickly to increase your energy levels.

14. EFT TAPPING

Emotions can and do get trapped in all our Meridians so the Guides attached, are only a guide. You have the freedom to use this tool as you are drawn to. As you begin to understand your own energy system, you will realise communication comes to you from all over your senses. People, places, events, colours, sounds, smells, will start to come to your attention as you Tap.

If it is a vivid memory, colourful and vibrant, still after all this time, trust that what comes to you is there to be cleared even if you don't fully understand why.

This is where you really start to tune into you and all that you are. You are energy in your own unique way, help it flow effectively. You have now progressed onto the sensory EFT Technique.

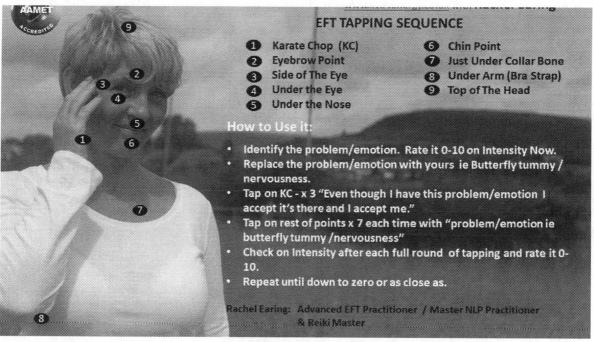

EFT TAPPING SEQUENCE

1. Karate Chop (KC)
2. Eyebrow Point
3. Side of The Eye
4. Under the Eye
5. Under the Nose
6. Chin Point
7. Just Under Collar Bone
8. Under Arm (Bra Strap)
9. Top of The Head

How to Use it:

- Identify the problem/emotion. Rate it 0-10 on Intensity Now.
- Replace the problem/emotion with yours ie Butterfly tummy / nervousness.
- Tap on KC - x 3 "Even though I have this problem/emotion I accept it's there and I accept me."
- Tap on rest of points x 7 each time with "problem/emotion ie butterfly tummy /nervousness"
- Check on Intensity after each full round of tapping and rate it 0-10.
- Repeat until down to zero or as close as.

Rachel Earing: Advanced EFT Practitioner / Master NLP Practitioner & Reiki Master

- Tap on your Karate Chop point (Soft Side of hand – See EFT chart for points) and say: General symptoms or target exactly how you are feeling and use those.
- Karate Chop: Say "Even though I have all these feelings all over my body I accept that they are there and I accept me"

  "Even though I have all these feelings all over my body I accept that they are there and I accept me anyway." Repeat x 2
- Tap on a Short Circuit of the flowing points repeating these short phrases

Top of eyebrow:	All these Feelings
Side of Eye:	All over my body

Under eye:	All these Feelings
Under Nose:	All over my body
On Chin:	All these feelings
Under Collar Bone:	All over my body
Under Arm:	All these feelings
Top of The Head:	All these feelings

Take a measure of how you are feeling in intensity with 10 being the highest and 0 being the lowest and repeat again to get as low as possible.

This system helps to raise to the surface issues/events/people which may need more detailed work on. As this happens be aware this is a natural process and clear as appropriate.

Repeat the above script and replace the Feeling with how you are now feeling and where these feelings are located.

IE: Even though my chest feels very tight and uncomfortable when I think of what. I accept that's how I feel and I accept me anyway.

Repeat x 2 and then go into short circuit using points above and shortend scripts:

"Chest feel tight"

"Uncomfortable

"When I think of that"

Assess again intensity 10-0 and repeat as necessary to lower.

15. TYPICAL EFT TECHNIQUE

1) If you know, you are feeling a particular emotion such as Jealousy / Longing / Shame use the Karate Chop point (Side of Hand) to start Tapping on and use the set up phrase.

   "Even though I have felt Jealous, Longing or Shame at "that" (let "that" represent the event or person you're thinking of) I understand these emotions are in the whole of my Energy system. Thank you for looking after me and when I'm ready I'll know when to let you go" repeat upto 3 times if necessary

2) Then work through a short Sequence of Tapping points as per Safety Method. Measure 10-0 of intensity and repeat as necessary

Short Sequence:

Top of Eyebrow	Jealous, Longing
Side of Eye:	Jealous, Longing,
Under Eye:	Shame, I'll Decide
Under Nose:	Shame, I'll Decide
On Chin:	Jealous, Longing
Underneath Collar Bone:	Jealous, Longing
Under Arm:	Shame I'll Decide

This system helps to raise to the surface issues/events/people which may need more detailed work on. As this happens be aware this is a natural process and clear as appropriate.

Keep clearing using all your senses really tune into your energy system and clear accordingly.

16. INNER AND OUTER BEAUTY

This is one is pure indulgence. It can be done on yourself on someone your care about. Some therapists will say this is dumbing down the depth of what EFT offers but frankly if it gets you starting to clear out your system and this is all you fancy USE IT.

Have to hand the following:
- ➢ Hot water
- ➢ Hand towels and flannels
- ➢ Organic Exfoliant
- ➢ Organic Face mask
- ➢ Organic Moisturiser
- ➢ Candles
- ➢ Relaxing music

Candles on, music on?

Get yourself comfortable and...

Quite simply, you now very gently give yourself a pressure point facial and hand massage, pressing and rubbing gently in a circular motion on each point on the face and fingers. Don't need to worry about the chest points down for this one but it's up to you.

You may do this with the intention of mentally asking for emotional clearance on each point or just enjoy the experience.
1) Set the room into a relaxing setting with the candles and music.
2) Set your chart so you are aware of each point to use **(optional)**
3) Dip a flannel in the hot water and gently wipe over your face. Add cleanser to remove dirt going over each tapping point and applying pressure gently as you cleanse, then wipe face.
4) Gently start to exfoliate your face gently going over each tapping point and applying gently pressure gently again as you cleanse.
5) Once completed again wipe your face with a clean hot flannel
6) Time to apply your face mask. Again gently using the tapping points and apply pressure gently as you start to apply your face mask.
7) Once your mask is applied, move to your hands and arms and rub the moisturiser gently into your hand and fingers. Applying gently circular pressure on each finger point.
8) As you go through this process you may be aware of how each point is reacting with the rest of your body. Ie: bladder, gall bladder and stomach point may make your tummy gurgle, or even cough etc as its opposite your lung meridian.

9) Each point massaged will help release blockages so take your time and really enjoy this one.

10) Once you have completed your hands you may remove your face mask with a fresh damp warm flannel gently rub over the tapping points.

11) Finally complete the facial with your moisturiser and again gently give yourself a full face massage gently using circular movements over each point and down your neck. You may wish to include your Kidney meridian (Under collar Bone) and Thymus Gland (Centre of chest) but just take your time and enjoy it as you wish.

Finally, relax and enjoy a glass of water and note down any gurgles, burps and releases you may have had or in the next hour or day after this.

This is pure indulgence and still works to clear any small blockages... BLISS.

17. FREEDOM AND RESILIENCE

As you start to enjoy these techniques and the freedom and resilience they give you

– Experiment like I have but with care.

>   Remember, You are more powerful than you will ever imagine!
- Remember energy is infinite and you are Tapping using your own energy system. You will know what feels right and sounds right to clear things for you and works for you on a daily level.
- Play around and enjoy the process of getting to know yourself on a vibrational level and when you're ready for a deep cleanse use a Practitioner to help you and give you more insight into techniques you may not be familiar with.
- You may just use one or two tapping points each day that's fine.
- As with anything the more you use it the more you will discover.

Enjoy the process...... and please give us your feedback.

FIVE STAR RATINGS ★★★★★

How has it helped others?

"In such a short space of time you have taught us so much and already made a huge difference in our lives.

As a family we are now using the tapping techniques you have taught us for sleep, de-stressing and improving our communication - which in itself has been a lovely bonus.

The thing that myself and my husband have found the most astounding is the powerful effect it has had with sleep. With an autistic, very anxious daughter on sleep medication which was no longer working, we now have a happier, less anxious daughter, that now sleeps within 30 minutes of going to bed. She is also using the techniques independently to get through the school day, which is lovely to see".

(H Ewens - Independent Business Owner)

"I've had one session with Rachel and she has changed my life in the most positive way! I've had 2/3 years of on and off radiotherapy and chemotherapy and although the effects of these were expected I also struggled with how I thought about what was happening and this in turn made the effects even worse. Rachel has shown me how to think differently and how to get rid of negativism, I have just completed a 6 week course of radiotherapy and although the tiredness has been there I have felt so different than the last time, I'm now ok that I may need to rest and I'm comfortable knowing that I have limitations and I must listen to my body.

Instead of feeling upset and angry about what is going on I can now say to myself 'its ok that you feel that way'. It has been one of the best things I have ever done and I cannot thank Rachel enough. I now use my tapping even sat at work when I'm having a moment of stress and it works beautifully."

Chloe (Training Manager/mum of 3)

"Much more powerful than I thought it would. I'm using the techniques on my 1 year old and would recommend any mums to give it a try". *(Hannah)*

"Rachel helped me with my migraines. I now do tapping where I need to."

(Claire – International Textile Designer)

If you have enjoyed this hand book you may be interested in undertaking the ETIS Programme with Rachel Earing, Live4Energy.

<u>THE ETIS PROGRAMME</u> (Engage, Transform, Inspire, Sustain)

Committing to relationships or work responsibilities is something which is expected of most of us, at some point in our life. Unfortunately, we often do not have the emotional resilience to deal with the challenges which occur during these experiences. Either we have never been taught how to deal with them effectively or we have become too full from our own experiences to take on anyone else's life pressures.

As this book explains there are many ways of starting this process off.

Feeling safe is one of our main primary emotions and when we do not feel safe this is when our fight, flight and freeze mechanism kicks in and we begin to feel anxious and on edge.

Imagine starting a relationship with someone and their past experiences trigger behaviour which constantly makes you and your relationship feel unsafe.

Imagine giving a project to someone you know is going through a very messy divorce with 3 teenage kids kicking off in the background, or this colleague is suffering from anxiety and depression because their loved ones or them, are suffering from a debilitating illness. Does this make you feel secure that the work will be a priority?

How wonderful would it be to know that you and the person you are about to embark on this relationship with, has already made a commitment of care to themselves to clear their own past triggers, whether that be in a personal relationship or a professional one?

How wonderful would it be to know that they are capable of recognizing old patterns of behaviour and can go and do something about it, or are less likely to "kick off" if you gently mention to them this might need clearing?

Imagine giving our children these tools so they don't have to carry around all the triggers (baggage) we've had for so many years.

What difference do you imagine it may make to their lives and the relationships they form in life?

Imagine having this available to your whole family and are able to experience this process together? (Not necessarily all at the same time, just in the same timescale.)

Yes, absolutely! It will be challenging! Probably the biggest challenge ever faced!

I wonder though, will it be more rewarding to watch each other suffer in their own unique way, through drinking, drugs, anger, anxiety, panic attacks, pain, depression, and then frustrated and confused again at each new trigger that appears in their life, possibly even frightened of themselves?

Or, will it be more rewarding to communicate more fully with each other, work at it together, be more understanding together, more loving together, more compassionate together, more resilient together?

What would we all be able to achieve with this in our lives?

How might it inspire others?

Why would YOU want to do this?

When would it begin?

Live4Energy offers a fully Evaluated & Certificated Bespoke Programme, plus a Standard Programme, which covers Individual or Group work on Emotional & Physical Health issues over a flexible 10 month period.

This certificate guarantees an individual has undertaken a commitment of care to themselves and you, (if it's your partner, family or business colleague). That they have started the process of self- responsibility in clearing old issues and gained new skills to recognize how to continue to do so.

These are some of the understandings you may experience.
- **Understanding your own Emotional and Physical Triggers**
- **How to do something about them yourself.**
- **Being more responsible with your reactions and behaviour.**
- **Understanding of how to uncover hidden beliefs systems.**
- **Breaking Down how Physical Pain impacts on your mental health**
- **How to Release Child Traumas and trauma in general.**
- **Breaking Down Resistance to Change**
- **Breaking Down Anxiety & Stress**
- **Empowering Self Confidence / Self Worth**
- **Skills for Life to deal with Lifes' Challenge**
- **Making space for the new adventures in life.**

If you'd like to book a course or gift it to someone you care about get in touch.

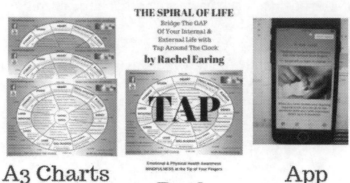

A3 Charts Book App

www.live4energy.co.uk

My journey from conception to realisation. Dreams can and do come true!
You just have to take ACTION.

Reference Material:

Dr Joe Dispenza – Being Supernatural

Bruce H Lipton (HD)- Biology Of Belief / Wisdom of Our Cells / Spontaneity of Evolution
David Feinstein, Donna Eden & Gary Craig – The Healing Power of EFT & Energy Psychology
Deepak Chopra, David Simon - Training The Mind, Healing The Body

Donna Eden, David Feinstein - Energy Medicine Masaru Emoto – The Hidden Messages In Water

Neale Donald Walsch – Conversations With God Awaken The Species Rhonda Byrne - The Secret

Ruby Wax - How To Be Human with a Neuroscientist & A Monk Tania A Prince - Mindfulness Based Inner Repatterning

Yuval Noah Harari: Sapiens: Homo Deus, A Brief History of Mankind

Printed in the United States
By Bookmasters